A Woman from God's Perspective

Anna Mary Byler

Vision Publishers
P.O. Box 190
Harrisonburg, VA 22803

First Edition 1999
Second Printing 2000

ISBN: 0-9717054-6-1

All Scripture quotations are taken from the King James Version.

Published by Vision Publishers, Inc.
Harrisonburg, Virginia

Cover Design: Lonnie D. Yoder

For additional copies or comments write to:
Vision Publishers, Inc.
P.O. Box 190
Harrisonburg, Virginia 22803
or Fax 1-540-432-6530
(See order forms in back)

Anyone wishing to write the author may do so at:
1200 Cold Springs Road
Stuarts Draft, Virginia 24477
Phone: 540-337-1190

A Woman from God's Perspective

Anna Mary Byler

Vision Publishers
P.O. Box 190
Harrisonburg, VA 22803

©1999 Anna Mary (Mrs. Bennie) Byler

First Edition 1999
Second Printing 2000

ISBN: 0-9717054-6-1

Attempt has been made to secure permission for the use of all copyrighted material. We have reason to believe some of these poems were written in the early nineteenth century and, therefore, are in public domain. We welcome any information which will help rectify any needed reference or credits.

All Scripture quotations are taken from the King James Version.

Published by Vision Publishers, Inc.
Harrisonburg, Virginia

Cover Design: Lonnie D. Yoder

For additional copies or comments write to:
Vision Publishers, Inc.
P.O. Box 190
Harrisonburg, Virginia 22803
or Fax 1-540-432-6530
(See order forms in back)

Anyone wishing to write the author may do so at:
1200 Cold Springs Road
Stuarts Draft, Virginia 24477
Phone: 540-337-1190

Table of Contents

Author's Note

In all of my writings, it is always my prayer and desire to give credit where credit is due. I cannot always be sure whether I have quoted directly from someone or not. My tutors have been many, and my head is full of things that have become "mine" as I try to live by them, but their sources may long be forgotten.

One thing, however, I am quite sure, I have nothing that I have not received. "A [person] can receive nothing except it be given . . . from heaven" (John 3:27). "And what hast thou that thou didst not receive?" (I Corinthians 4:7). Nothing that I present in these pages is new or original, but I trust it is faithfully Scriptural, and can be to the praise and glory of God.

Those who see God's
hand in everything
can best leave every-
thing in God's hand

Acknowledgements

I am deeply indebted to:

My loving heavenly Father, who has been so faithful through all generations. I am keenly aware that I am nothing of myself. If this book is a blessing to others it is because of God. "What hast thou that thou didst not receive?" (I Corinthians 4:7).

My faithful husband, Bennie, my children and grandchildren. They add so much to my life and experience. Especially to Sharon, a busy mother of three, for doing the calligraphy for the cover of the book. And Shirley, for typing the manuscript and designing the cover.

Those who took time to read the manuscript and offer helpful suggestions.

Simon Schrock for writing the preface.

James Goering for the final review of the manuscript.

Campbell Copy and especially Anita Rhodes for their encouragement, patience and for the finished product.

"I may have written, others shared their thoughts and suggestions, Shirley may have done the typing, Brother James may have done the final proofreading, but it is God who gives the increase."

(I Corinthians 3:6 – paraphrased)

Not I,
but Christ !

Gal. 2:20

Introduction

From God's perspective, the most precious thing is the preservation of His people. They have come to put their confidence and competence in Him, are under His control, are overwhelmed by His love, and are trusting Him completely.

In response to such compassion and care, there springs up within my soul an overflowing stream of gratitude. "O my God, how great Thou art! O my Heavenly Father, how wondrous are Your ways! The truth of this is tremendously touching. It strips away any pride or arrogance, because it is You, O God, who lives within my heart and who leads me into becoming a *Woman from Your Perspective*."

I have been through some hard times, both physically and emotionally. Through it all, God's grace and His never-ending love have always been sufficient. It is my heartfelt desire to live for His glory and to bring pleasure to the heart of my Father.

Perspective, according to Webster, means the capacity to view things in their true relation or relative importance.

Contentment is the hallmark of the woman who views life from God's perspective, and who desires to live always with His perspective as her goal.

Since she lives from God's perspective, she lives in the security of her heavenly Father. She radiates a serene confidence and quiet joy that surmounts all the tragedies that come into her life.

Instead of questioning why the sickness, or tragedy, she reflects on God's past faithfulness. Her faith is increased as she leans on Him today and trusts Him for all her tomorrows.

She lives in the quiet assurance that God has what is best for her in mind. Therefore, she does not fear the pain, suffering, or disappointments that may become her lot. Rather, she focuses on God's many promises. This brings a quiet and peaceful joy that surpasses all earthly sorrow.

As you read these pages, it is my prayer that you will open your heart, lift your eyes to Jesus, and find peace. You will learn to see from God's perspective, as your heart is pure and as you love to obey Him cheerfully, promptly, and completely.

With the desire to be a woman from God's perspective, comes the commitment to be sensitive to His gentle Holy Spirit and to obey instantly His smallest wish.

I will wait quietly as He unfolds His purpose and plan. In harmony, unity, and peace, God and I commune together throughout the day. He is my Shepherd, my most intimate companion. More than that, God is my life!

Preface

Life isn't all everblooming roses. The bright petals fall and the thorns prick our comfort zones. The future is lined with scattered clouds of uncertainty.

A Woman From God's Perspective comes at a time of rapid change in how we work and live. Our impressive technology is constantly improved, forcing us to update or replace. City dumps are peppered with obsolete electronic equipment. The housewife has an abundance of automatic gadgets to "save time" and do her work, and the advertisers advise her that she still doesn't have the latest.

However, with the ever changing conveniences comes the longing for purpose and contentment. There is a need for lasting values and security that doesn't change.

This book is written from a heart's desire to draw encouragement and direction from the solid lasting truth of God's Word. It cites time-proven principles to give guidance through an ungodly culture.

The author writes in the midst of her own testing and suffering. She writes from the experience of a loyal wife, a faithful mother and a caring grandmother. Her insights come from a deep inner desire to be <u>A Woman From God's Perspective</u>, a commitment to God's Word and a careful walk with Him.

Here is a noteworthy encouragement to be a godly person in a changing world.

Simon Schrock

Beatitudes of the Devotional Life

Blessed is the person who daily reads God's Word, for he shall not be wanting in knowing God's will.

Blessed is the one who daily prays alone to God, for his faith in the heavenly Father shall increase more and more.

Blessed is the person who meditates on God's Word and works, for he shall be filled with awe and amazement at the wondrous plan of God.

Blessed is the person who meets God first in the morning, for he shall have an unseen Companion with him all the day.

Blessed is the person who daily confesses his need and dependence on God, for he shall be helped and sustained in due time.

Blessed is the person who anticipates a devotional experience with God, for he shall be rewarded an hundred fold.

Blessed is the person who personally worships God, for he shall find fulfillment and the best in life.

Blessed is the person who personally honors Christ, for he shall experience the length and breadth and the height and depth of love.

Blessed is the person who personally is filled with the Holy Spirit, for he shall bear the perfect fruit of love, joy, peace, patience, kindness, goodness, faithfulness, gentleness, and self-control.

--Aaron Lapp, Jr., 1979
Used by permission

1

Around-the-Clock Worship

To really know Jesus Christ as Savior and Lord is to love and worship Him continually.

As God's children, we are often confused about worship. We are prone to think of worship as something we do when we go to church. We call the church building God's house, because it was dedicated to Him when the building was completed. So we continue with the confusing idea it must be the only place to worship.

Sunday, the first day of the week, is the day Jesus met with His disciples. It has become the Christian's day of rest (Luke 24:1; 1 Corinthians 16:2). It is to be set aside to give Him our full devotion and adoration, and to rest from our daily pursuits. God set an example of working for six days. Then He rested on the seventh. "And he rested on the seventh day from all his work which he had made" (Genesis 2:2).

The difference between worship on Sunday and the rest of the week is that Sunday is set aside to give God our full attention through reading His Word, singing, and listening to His Word proclaimed. This is to prepare us to worship Him properly around-the-clock.

The Bible says "Ye are the temple of the living God . . . I will dwell in them, and walk in them; and I will be their

1

God, and they shall be my people" (2 Corinthians 6:16). God's dwelling place is in the heavens, but He also desires to live and work in the pure and holy heart.

"For thus saith the high and lofty One . . . I dwell in the high and holy place, with him also that is of a contrite and humble spirit" (Isaiah 57:15).

Brother Lawrence, as revealed in the book, *The Practice of the Presence of God*, is a classic example of one who lived a life of continual worship. This book consists of letters and bits of conversations of a humble, yet exalted, lay brother who lived in the year 1666. After his conversion at the age of eighteen, he was known as a strong Christian. His goal from there on was "to walk as in His presence."[1]

His work found him in the monastery kitchen among the clatter of pots and pans, yet he served God effectively. He demonstrated by his life, how at any moment and in any circumstance, the soul that seeks God may find Him and experience living in His presence. "The time of business," said he, "does not with me differ from the time of prayer; and in the noise and commotion of my kitchen while several persons are at the same time calling for different things, I possess God in as great tranquillity as if I were upon my knees at the blessed sacraments" (page 30, *The Practice of the Presence of God*).

Around-the-clock worship can best be described as to be always with God. Remember, no one can hide from God's all-seeing eye (read Psalm 139), no one can get away from God's presence. What a blessing it is to always enjoy being in His presence. To do nothing, to say nothing, or even to think nothing that would displease Him is the

---

[1]Fleming H. Revell, Published by Spire Books, Baker Book House Co. P.O. Box 6287, Grand Rapids, MI 49516-6287.

acceptable worship that glorifies God around the clock. This is only possible, though, as we love God with all our heart. "Thou shalt love the Lord thy God with all thy heart, and with all thy soul, and with all thy mind" (Matthew 22:37).

In order to experience a life of God-approved worship, the heart must be cleansed and free from all other affections. "Set your affection [mind] on things above, not on things on the earth. For ye are dead, and your life is hid with Christ in God" (Colossians 3:2, 3). The mind that is stayed upon God is a singular mind. It is not in conflict with other passions. Since our God is a jealous God, He will possess the heart alone. He will not share His residence with any other affections. "For thou shalt worship no other god: for the LORD whose name is Jealous, is a jealous God" (Exodus 34:14).

A thankful heart is where God dwells. "In every thing give thanks: for this is the will of God" (1 Thessalonians 5:18a). A thankful heart will be content to accept the surroundings and situations that cannot be changed.

There is no time or place for murmuring and complaining. Instead of focusing on the negative, the focus must be on God, the center of attraction. Therefore, when the sun is hidden behind dark, thundering clouds, there will still be a reverence and worship that pleases God, because God is good and doesn't change. In every life there are bound to be days and trials as dark as the darkest night. But if our eyes are on Jesus, the heart will remain thankful and grateful to God the Giver, rather than focusing on whether God blesses or not.

God will at times permit disease in the body in order to cleanse and cure the diseases of the soul. Even in sickness God desires to be worshiped, knowing we are all-dependent on Him. The worst affliction never is intolerable, unless we view it in the wrong light. If we see affliction as permitted by God, suffering will lose its bitterness and become our consolation, because we realize God loves us and is refining our lives. Suffering is also a means to bring us into a deeper, more satisfying relationship with Him.

The more a person recognizes his unworthiness, the more he will consciously rely on God; and that is part of worship. The greater perfection a soul aspires after, the more dependent he is on divine grace.

From a thankful heart stems a diligence that desires to please God in everything. "Whatsoever ye do in word or deed, do all in the name of the Lord Jesus, giving thanks . . ." (Colossians 3:17). "Whatsoever thy hand findeth to do, do it with thy might" (Ecclesiastes 9:10). "And whatsoever ye do, do it heartily, as to the Lord" (Colossians 3:23). "For it is God which worketh in you both to will and to do of his good pleasure" (Philippians 2:13).

When worship becomes an around-the-clock attitude, it will make a difference in how we respond to disruptions in our schedule, and the frustrations God allows to come our way, to test us and to try our hearts. "Not as pleasing men, but God, which trieth our hearts" (1 Thessalonians 2:4b).

In sickness and accidents it becomes obvious whether or not we experience around-the-clock worship.

The reward of continual worship is that God is sensitive to our cry in direct proportion to our sensitivity to Him. When we worship God around the clock, whether we feel like it or not, we experience two things. First, we bring joy to God because of our obedience, which brings peace to our hearts. Secondly, we bring light into a dark world. These provide opportunities for turning others to the knowledge of the only true God Who is worthy of around-the-clock worship.

True worship
springs
from a
Pure heart!

Soaring

Sometimes God takes away our props
that we might lean on Him,
allows temptation, so we'll grow
and triumph over sin.

Sometimes He takes away our strength
for doing earthly things
to rest our bodies that our souls
may soar on eagle wings.

Let's not resent it when He says,
"Come ye apart – Be still"
or chafe at disappointments
that are His sovereign will.

Oh, let's not doubt or question "Why?"
with unexplained delays,
but keep on soaring 'neath His wings
with gratitude and praise!

--Alice H. Martenson
Source Unknown

2

Recounting God's Faithfulness

As we approach the beginning of another year, we do not know what lies ahead. It is difficult, if not impossible, to anticipate all that may transpire within the next twelve months.

More than likely, all of us will experience changes and situations that we could not handle if God in His faithfulness would not withhold these scenes from us. They would rob us of the joy of a restful night. If we knew there was a cloud of adversity waiting for us just around the corner, we could not see the excellent creation around us, the beautiful sunrise, the delightful and serene sunset, and the little eye-appealing, eye-filling beauties of everyday living.

To some there may be unexpected illnesses, accidents, or even death. Such possibilities do not need to strike fear or anxiety in our hearts. Rather, it should be a security to know that every moment is in the hands of our great God, the Omnipresent, Omniscient, and Omnipotent One! In Psalm 39:4, David gives us a true description of our life, "LORD, make me to know mine end, and the measure of my days, what it is; that I may know how frail I am."

The Amplified Bible would indicate we must remember

7

God and appreciate the privilege of living, and how transient our stay here is. The New International Version reads: "Show me, O LORD, my life's end . . . let me know how fleeting is my life."

Every event, whether disappointing or thrilling, painful or joyful, is all part of God's purposeful arrangement for our fulfillment. In fact, these events, if we accept them as God's will, can be the entrance to "joy unspeakable and full of glory" (1 Peter 1:8). We will find this true as we view every experience from God's vantage point.

In order to be victorious during pain and suffering we must be aware of God's presence, power, and approval. Then we can say with Jeremiah, "The LORD is with me" (Jeremiah 20:11a).

We can rest in God's faithfulness that no accident, no assignment, nothing – absolutely nothing – touches me that has not first passed God's approval. Events don't just happen. They are monitored by God to bring us into the conformity of His dear Son. "That I may know him, and the power of his resurrection, and the fellowship of his sufferings, being made conformable unto his death" (Philippians 3:10).

In light of my experiences through the past year with regard to my health, I have been made aware repeatedly of the uncertainty of life and the importance of keeping my focus on Jesus. I do deeply appreciate recovery and healing along with numerous blessings, but I have a greater anticipation and desire for Jesus' return. Instead of enjoying summer activities, I needed to accept a slower pace of life. God's faithfulness was the grace I received to change my plans and enjoy the little so often unnoticed beauties of nature.

For several months, a regular appointment with the chiropractor relieved the severe pain caused by a pinched nerve. Learning the art of contentment was needful. I learned "in whatsoever state I am, therewith to be content" (Philippians 4:11). During the past year God permitted other infirmities to enter my usual healthy, energetic body.

On a number of different occasions, I would get sick and have severe pain in my abdomen. I would be flat on my back for several days at a time. Often I would ask God to help me be an easy learner of this school of life. The song, "Lord, whatever it takes to draw closer to Thee, that's what I'll be willing to do" became my theme as I faced some uncertainties.

One Saturday morning, instead of the pain vanishing, it became excruciating and brought on vomiting and fainting. I needed to see a doctor. On the way, I felt too sick to go to the doctor's office, so we went to the emergency room. After about six hours and several pain shots, I felt better. Tests did not reveal any reason for the pain. I was permitted to go home with antibiotics and pain pills, but Monday morning I felt worse. A CT scan revealed diverticulosis, an abscess in my colon. I was admitted to the hospital for five days because intravenous infusion was necessary. When I was released the surgeon told me he had expected to do emergency surgery. Again, I was made aware of the faithfulness of God. Emergency surgery would mean a colostomy until the infection cleared up. How I praised God for His blessings as I left the hospital. It was easy to submit to a very strict diet. This affected my efficiency, but I felt too grateful to God for His faithfulness to complain. So, instead, I focused on God's goodness to me.

The Saturday morning when I got so deathly sick, I didn't know if I would be facing death. I didn't know if I'd ever come back to my home and grandchildren (three were there for breakfast when I left). I could say I felt I was ready to meet my Maker, but God in His faithfulness brought me through this experience. God permits pain in order to refine and purify. As I was going through these experiences, I often prayed that God would refine and purge me to make me a purer vessel and channel for His service.

Someone once said, "Either we resist or surrender to suffering, and to surrender means total abandonment." Which we choose depends on our attitude towards God. Immediate surrender brings joy and freedom to learn what God is teaching in the midst of suffering.

During the time of my painful experience, we were in the process of adding a front porch to our small house of thirty-three years. Instead of this being a small undertaking as we had expected, it became a major project. Repairs had to be made. Galvanized water pipes needed to be replaced with plastic ones. Unfortunately, the well is located in the front yard. That meant digging trenches all through the lawn.

Monday morning when Bennie and I were leaving for the tests, the trenches needed to be covered so we could get out our drive. As we were leaving, I told Bennie, "Look at the lawn, that is how I feel inside. All torn up!" Through it all I felt a peace, knowing God was in control.

Ron Hamilton so aptly penned a few lines of a song, "God never moves without purpose or plan when trying His servants and molding a man." I did not need to understand; God was only asking us to hold His hand and be faithful. He was faithful. He had proven faithful so many times, and I was confident He would not disappoint me now.

There were some anxious moments. At times I would suddenly have an attack, but again it was God's faithfulness that kept me healthy until I could have surgery three months later.

A year earlier, I had been involved in an automobile accident. I suffered a severe hematoma. I was still under doctors care when a mammogram revealed calcium deposits forming, so I was scheduled to have a surgical biopsy as an outpatient. Tests returned benign, and I was reminded again of God's faithfulness.

Everyone faces a certain amount of fear of the unknown. God's faithfulness in past experiences strengthens faith to trust Him more completely in present and future difficulties.

Those three months of strict diet, antibiotics, doctor appointments, and checkups were all under God's providence. Submitting with a contented heart and a thankful spirit proved a blessing to my family, especially to the grandchildren. The time of waiting and not knowing whether God would permit me a scheduled surgery or an emergency surgery was a test of faith. God in His goodness allowed me to look forward to the day when I could return to normal living, to a normal diet, and to not always feeling so exhausted.

As fall approached, the lawn was green and complete again, and new shrubs put the finishing touch around the beautiful front porch and walks.

I did spend nine days in the hospital. My surgery was successful. I was deeply thankful for God's faithfulness, as I recovered and enjoyed visitors and especially the family and grandchildren.

On either side of my hospital room were very sick ladies who had had emergency surgery. When I left the hospital, the head nurse said, "You are fortunate. Both of your next door neighbors will be leaving with colostomies." Not only was I fortunate, I was richly blessed!

Yes, it is through our deepest waters, those hottest fires, those darkest valleys, that God desires to teach us the most blessed and the most eternal lessons.

As I reflect on my trials the past two years I see God indeed has been faithful. This does give me grace and strength to trust Him completely with the present, and to place my hand in His hand for all my tomorrows.

Confidence
in God is the
hope that keeps
us from despair.

God Knows And He Cares

Each little part of our life,
Or burdens hard to bear,
God knows about them all,
And surely he does care.

The little sparrow does not fall,
Unnoticed by his loving gaze,
How much more he cares for us,
And knowingly plans our days.

He knows the winding path,
He calls on us to trod,
But never ever will we be,
Forsaken by our God.

His ways are far beyond ours,
He knows what is for our good,
So even if we don't understand,
Let's trust him as we should.

Because he cares for us,
We need never fear,
His love surrounds our lives,
And he is always near.

He's near to bless and guide,
He's near to hold our hand,
And when his purpose is fulfilled,
He'll bring us home to Gloryland.

Miriam Chupp
used by permission, 1999

3

Is Brokenness
Really a Blessing?

The story is told of an architect who ordered a number of gigantic mirrors to grace the walls of the Royal Palace of Teheran. When they arrived they were cracked. The frustrated and disappointed engineer ordered them to be trashed.

When it was reported to the architect, he commanded the broken fragments to be recovered. Then he requested the pieces of mirrors to be crushed into tiny bits. He then glued these to the wall and ceiling of the palace where they glistened like diamonds.

God, too, is an architect. He has a beautiful plan for every life that is willing to be broken if that is what will bring more glory to God.

There may be times when we feel we are doing our very best and we feel God blessing. But sometimes instead of goodwill and physical successes, we encounter trials and afflictions.

There have been times in my life when I felt like shattered fragments of glass. I wondered what good could develop from my broken and crushed life. But Peter's words jolted me to the realization that we are not to think it

15

strange when we meet with trials and crushing experiences. But rather we are to "rejoice, inasmuch as ye are partakers of Christ's suffering; that when his glory shall be revealed, ye may be glad also with exceeding joy" (1 Peter 4:12 & 13).

I came to grips with the thought that I can fret and fume and wallow in self-pity and question God's goodness. Or I can ask God to keep me from doubting, and know that His love is eternal and "underneath are the everlasting arms" (Deuteronomy 33:27b). Affliction can become a blessing in disguise when we allow God to break our self-will. Trials are always used by God to refine our lives.

In John 12:24, Jesus used the analogy of the seed that must die in order to produce other seed and eventually yield a rich harvest. "Except a corn of wheat fall into the ground and die, it abideth alone: but if it die, it bringeth forth much fruit."

This process is known as brokenness – when self dies and God's will becomes our sole desire. The outer shell must break in order for the new life in Christ to emerge. Only then can one's life become useful.

Job is a good example of one who was walking close to God. The Bible describes him as irreproachable. Nothing could be said against him. He was honest and held high the codes of right behavior. He had a reverent fear of God and he avoided even looking at evil deliberately and habitually. He was known as the greatest man in all his time, yet his family was his first priority. He offered sacrifices and prayers daily just in case one of his children sinned.

The story is recorded in the book of Job. God allowed Satan to afflict him. In one day all his wealth was stolen, thieves drove his animals away, and his children were killed. Yet, Job was able to say, "The LORD gave and the

LORD hath taken away; blessed be the name of the Lord" (Job 1:21). Verse 22 says, "In all this Job sinned not, nor charged God foolishly."

Job knew God; therefore, he could say, "But he knoweth the way that I take: when he hath tried me, I shall come forth as gold" (Job 23:10).

King David experienced crushing times as well. Instead of indulging in self-pity, he declared, "The LORD is my shepherd; I shall not want" (Psalm 23:1). David's responses set an example for us to consider. Instead of dwelling on his problems, the psalmist took courage and comfort in God's love. I Samuel 30:6, says, "But David encouraged himself in the LORD." Instead of trying to drown his hurts in worldly pursuits, he found refuge in the Lord, "He that dwelleth in the secret place of the most High shall abide under the shadow of the Almighty. I will say of the LORD, He is my refuge and my fortress: my God; in him will I trust" (Psalm 91:1, 2). Instead of pursuing material gain, he placed his confidence in God's unchanging Word (read Psalm 15). Instead of complaining, he gave himself to praise, "Bless the LORD, O my soul: and all that is within me, bless his holy name" (Psalm 103:1).

The Bible gives us Peter for another example of one who thought he had his life all together. He was one of Jesus' disciples and very outspoken at times. During Jesus' betrayal, however, Peter followed afar off. Earlier he told Jesus that he would never desert Him and would even be willing to die with Him (Luke 22:33). Jesus needed to remind him that before the rooster would crow, Peter would deny Him three times (John 18:15-17). After Peter denied the LORD, he went out into the night and wept bitterly (Luke 22:62). This is where Peter repented and became a broken, humble Peter.

After Jesus' resurrection, He had another conversation with Peter. Since Peter denied Jesus three times, Jesus asked him the question three times, "Simon . . . lovest thou me?" When Jesus asked Peter the third time, he was no longer the same confident Peter, but now he replied by saying, "Lord, thou knowest all things; thou knowest that I love thee" (John 21:17). Because Peter was a broken Peter, he became a Spirit-filled Peter. Because Peter did not allow his flesh preeminence, God's Spirit now moved into his heart and he became a useful man of God.

Peter experienced failure when he did not keep his promise. He also experienced loss when Jesus was crucified. Jesus knew what it would take to break Peter's outer shell so that his life would be poured out and able to bless many lives. Peter is a good example of the beauty of brokenness. He experienced the seed falling into the ground and decaying. His life reveals the true secret of a broken life.

Brokenness is a process. It was so in Peter's life. His denial and the Lord's reproachful look was the crushing experience. Yet Peter experienced a continual breaking and purging. The product of the brokenness was a man that God could use. He was the man who at Pentecost preached repentance to three thousand souls (Acts 2). He was the writer of I & II Peter. Peter was used of God to heal a lame man (Acts 3:1-11). While he was asleep in prison, an angel woke him and led him through locked doors to freedom. He truly demonstrated by his life the absolute necessity of brokenness.

God knows that it's the heart that must be broken because that is where the strength is. God strikes where the strength lies.

Joseph's life story, found in Genesis 37-47, gives us a

good picture of the process of brokenness that was a real blessing. In all the afflictions and rejection Joseph experienced he never despaired. Rather, he kept God in focus. The phrase "the Lord blessed Joseph" or "the Lord was with him" is found about six times in this account. Hosts of people and animals were spared during the seven years of famine because of Joseph's faithful spirit. All through his life, he was willing to allow God to crush him and break the outer shell of his self-life, so that the product of brokenness could bless others. Only a Spirit-filled Joseph could truly forgive his brothers for the jealousy, envy, and hatred that he had experienced. And only a Spirit-filled Joseph could truly say from his heart, "'But as for you, ye thought evil against me; but God meant it unto good' . . . And he comforted them, and spake kindly unto them" (Genesis 50:20 & 21b).

Ron Hamilton penned these fitting words, "God never moves without purpose or plan, when trying his servant and molding a man. Give thanks to the Lord, though your testing seems long; In darkness He giveth a song."

When I realize brokenness as an instrument of blessing, I will allow God complete control. With that assurance I will acknowledge Him as Creator as well as He who promised never to leave me or forsake me (Hebrews 13:5).

May my life eventually become a demonstration that it is possible to allow God to break my outer shell in order that brokenness can really become a blessing.

The Greatest of All

"And thou shalt love the Lord thy God with all thy heart, and with all thy soul, and with all thy mind, and with all thy strength: this is the first commandment. And the second is like, namely this, Thou shalt love thy neighbour as thyself. . ." (Mark 12:30 & 31).

The Bible has the answer to every problem we face personally or in our family setting.

Following are seven guidelines for a happy, fulfilled, and meaningful life:

1. Commit yourself daily, hourly, to the purpose of glorifying Jesus as Lord.
2. Spend time each day meditating on God's Word; then apply it to your life. Ask yourself, "What is God showing me in each situation?"
3. Check your thought life frequently. Get rid of mind arguing, grudges, and evil thoughts.
4. Spend time together as a family. Do your part to resolve family conflicts.
5. Share and appreciate good associates; share your joys and sorrows, your victories, trials and answered prayers.
6. Have a daily routine, including work, relaxation, and projects that need attention. This brings personal satisfaction, as well as renewed zeal to be organized.
7. Ask God to make you sensitive to needs around you.

Have a goal to encourage someone each day.

These are all ways that we show God whether or not we love Him with all our hearts, and then love our neighbors as ourselves.

By obeying the great commandment, we are also obeying all the other commandments!

Seven is the complete number. There are seven pillars that are needful in order to construct a home that will enhance the preciousness of children. Also seven guidelines, when followed, will make it easier for Mom and Dad to be sensitive to the needs of their precious children. Thereby they will be a joy and blessing to each other.

1. *They must focus on God. What would God want them to do in a situation? Through that mentality they will bring out the best in each other and also in their children.*

2. *They must regularly bathe their minds and hearts in the truth of God's Word. Immorality thrives on untruth and twisted concepts.*

3. *They must live discreetly when dealing or working with the opposite sex. They must always have a high respect and reverence for their marriage vows.*

4. *They must encourage each other to do their best in their abilities and skills. Usually they have opposite temperaments.*

5. *They must remember to weave little unnoticed courtesies into their busy schedule.*

6. *They must take their responsibility consistently, whether they feel like it or not.*

7. *They must develop the skill of an understanding heart. They must cultivate a high respect for each other. They must be able to share from their hearts by one listening while the other expresses himself.*

These seven points if followed develop and build a faithful spirit. Then building a home with the seven pillars will become easier.

4

Me, Be Perfect?

Mae enjoyed her daily quiet time with God. She had experienced many victories, and her love and commitment to her Lord was deep and devoted. One of her favorite passages was the Sermon on the Mount. She read and reread all the enriching instructions for the godly person. In one of her studies, the verse, "Be ye therefore perfect, even as your Father which is in heaven is perfect" (Matthew 5:48), gripped her heart. Her first response was, "Me, be perfect? I can never be perfect as God in heaven is perfect."

But, let us not forget that when God gives a requirement or command in His Word, He never leaves the honest seeker without an answer. Our perfect God has a perfect standard. Webster defines *perfect* as "faithfully reproducing the original." That makes it plain that it does mean me!

The Hebrew word indicates "to stand boldly out." We like to make excuses for our faults, shortcomings, and even sin and for not being perfect, but that is not Scriptural. "Be ye perfect" is not an option; it is a command. God calls us "to stand boldly out."

Down through the ages God sought out those who were perfect before Him. Noah was a just man and perfect in his generation. He walked with God (Genesis 6:9). Because Noah walked with God, he also found grace in the eyes of

23

God, (verse 8). Isn't that a blessed state to find ourselves in? Noah was in the minority, and yet he was able to live a holy life, perfect before God, while living in a generation of wickedness (verse 5).

When God called Abraham, he said "Here I am" (Genesis 22:1). Those words express the greatest application of the human mind. To say, "Here I am," when God calls is possible only when we walk perfectly in His presence, the only place where we can obey. To understand where I am in the sight of God means not only to listen, but to obey promptly. Abraham was called by God and God promised to make a covenant with him. In Genesis 17:1, God tells Abraham to "walk before me, and be thou perfect."

"Thou shalt be perfect with the LORD thy God" (Deuteronomy (18:13). God's people, the Israelites, were also called to be perfect.

Job, in Chapter 1, is referred to as "that man [who] was perfect and upright, and one that feared God . . ." These four references indicate that even in the beginning of time, God worked through those who were perfect, upright, and sincere.

In all four of these accounts, people were not without faults, but rather they possessed a perfect heart of obedience to God. God is not demanding perfect performance, but rather God is looking for a perfect heart – a heart that is upright and sincere, one that is sensitive and obedient, a heart that is mellow and teachable, caring and compassionate.

We also are reminded of several accounts of those whose hearts were not perfect toward God. King Solomon, the wisest king and the one who asked God for an understanding heart, allowed obstacles to dim his vision for a perfect heart. I Kings 11:4, "And his heart was not perfect with the LORD his God."

King Jeroboam also turned from having a perfect heart. I Kings 15:3b, "And his heart was not perfect with the Lord his God."

The testimony of King Amaziah was that "he did that which was right in the sight of the LORD, but not with a perfect heart" II Chronicles 25:2). This indicates that it is possible to live right, yet not with a perfect heart. It is only the perfect heart that pleases God. Anything less is not good enough.

In Matthew 23, the phrase, "Woe unto you, scribes and Pharisees, hypocrites" is recorded eight times. Jesus harshly condemned them in their pretense. They professed outwardly to be godly, but inwardly they were full of hypocrisy and iniquity (verse 28). They completely missed the conditions God required. God's command is to be perfect, and He is still looking for those whose hearts are perfect toward God. In all of God's doings in our lives, He is aiming at perfection of character.

Philippians 3:13-15 has the answer for the question, Can I really be perfect? "I count not myself to have apprehended: but this one thing I do, forgetting those things which are behind, and reaching forth unto those things which are before, I press toward the mark for the prize of the high calling of God in Christ Jesus. Let us therefore, as many as be perfect," do this!

Paul found the answer in Christ. Colossians 1:10-12: "That ye might walk worthy of the Lord unto all pleasing, being fruitful in every good work, and increasing in the knowledge of God; Strengthened with all might . . . Giving thanks unto the Father." We, like Paul, can also find the answer! II Timothy 3:16; 17: "All scripture is given by inspiration of God, and is profitable for doctrine, for reproof, for correction, for instruction in righteousness: That the [woman] of God may be perfect, throughly furnished unto all good works."

Jesus is our ultimate Example of a person who was perfect upon the earth. He was made perfect through obedience and suffering. We can learn so much about perfection by studying His life. He had a love and compassion for all people. He was continually subject and obedient to His Father's will.

"That we may present every man perfect in Christ Jesus" (Colossians 1:28).

"Let us go on to perfection" (Hebrews 6:1).

"Now the God of peace . . . make you perfect in every good work to do his will" (Hebrews 13:20, 21).

"That ye may be perfect and entire, wanting nothing" (James 1:4).

This command is found frequently in the New Testament and it is neither optional nor impossible. Perfection in Christ is both a state of being and a state of becoming. Perfection is the beginning of great potential for growth and maturity in Christ.

The message, "be perfect," demands the whole heart, the whole life, all our strength, and our mind. Our Father, who raised Jesus from the dead, is always ready, in the same resurrection power to perfect us to do His will.

Grace enables us
to do what we
cannot do
of ourselves.

Too Late

I rushed to town to the grocery store
For an item I'd forgotten before.
They're open till nine, it's eight-fifty-eight;
But the closed sign is out, I am too late.

I race to the airport to catch my plane.
As I run down the hall they call my name.
My bags are so heavy, surely they'll wait;
But the plane is leaving, I am too late!

It is Sunday morning, how the time flies!
We scamper and hurry and rub our eyes.
As we leave, I think, no more can I take!
I hear them singing; again we are late.

I wronged someone, I wounded a dear friend.
But opportunity's gone to amend,
For he has passed on through the pearly gate,
I'm filled with remorse that I was too late!

To tell my neighbor about that Great Day,
I had intended, now he's move away
I haven't seen him since and I berate
Myself that I wanted, now it's too late!

The trumpets are sounding, the clouds roll back.
Will you cry, "But wait! One thing I yet lack."
But, oh, my dear friend, you have sealed your fate;
Jesus will say, "You're forever too late!"

– Mrs. Ruth Weaver
used by permission 1999

5
The Octopus of Jealousy

The octopus is a sea animal with a soft body and eight arms called tentacles, reaching in all directions. Tentacles are flexible and grasp everything within reach.

The World Book calls the octopus "devil fish," perhaps because of its ugliness and also its power to camouflage. From the siphon it is able to squirt a black fluid that forms a dark cloud, causing other sea animals to lose sight of it.

One of our children was given a colorful octopus of yarn. When it was placed on a flat surface, it was very intriguing. Since the phrase, the octopus of jealousy, has been going around in my mind, and I discovered some of its definitions, it has lost its luster. A sticky substance that masters everything within its reach and the prison that entwines and crushes is not a beautiful picture. But isn't that a very good description of jealousy?

Jealousy often reaches in all directions. It conquers and masters all within its reach. It disguises itself and is often well hidden from human view. It appears as something harmless, but jealousy is like an octopus. It destroys with its eight tentacles, of pride, strife, criticism, envy, backbiting, gossip, selfishness, and covetousness.

Someone once said that *pride* is at the base root of all other sins. It is described as excessive self-conceit.

Strife means "to inflict pain." It can be done in several different ways, but most often it is inflicted by words. Proverbs reminds us of the power words carry. "He that hath knowledge spareth his words . . ." (Proverbs 17:27a).

Criticism is the opposite of encouragement. It undermines and is given to harsh and captious judgments.

Envy is an attitude of a painful or resentful awareness of an advantage enjoyed by another, joined with a desire to possess the same advantage at someone else's expense.

Backbiting relates to the speech, to say mean or spiteful things about another.

Gossip is identified as habitually revealing personal and sensational facts, or spreading exciting or confidential interests about others.

Selfishness concentrates on one's own advantage, pleasure, or well-being, without regard to the other. Self is the main object.

Covetousness desires what belongs to another. It exceeds unreasonable limits to acquire wealth and often at the expense of broken relationships.

All of these traits are carnal and bring bondage rather than the freedom and blessing that the person really desires. These are often recognized in the following attitudes:

1. Being discontent with the way God designed me.
2. Struggling with inferiority when I'm with knowledgeable people.
3. Discontent with my husband's occupation and financial means.
4. Dissatisfied with my cooking skills.
5. Complaining about my disorderly house.
6. Feeling inadequate around others who are more efficient.
7. Finding it difficult to communicate.

8. Feeling that no one cares.
9. My private devotions are dull and meaningless.
10. I feel useless and insignificant.
11. I feel depressed because I'm not needed.
12. Having a compulsion to do more and more.
13. I feel frustrated and irritable when other's lives seem in order.

But praise the Lord, no one needs to continue in these crippling characteristics. Rather, we need to acknowledge we have a problem. Only God can give a new heart and attitudes that please Him.

Since jealousy is a heart problem that affects our performance, we must bring self to the foot of the cross. Otherwise our energy is sapped, and finally we end up emotionally drained and bitter. When jealousy is brought to Jesus at the cross, our emotions will be healed and vitality renewed. Then we can experience peace and freedom to become all God has planned.

God's plan is for us to enjoy freedom in Christ.

When I am in Christ, self no longer is in control, but Christ lives in me (Galatians 2:20).

Through Jesus, God has received me as His child (John 1:12).

Christ has cleansed my slate; now I am justified before a holy God (Romans 5:1). It cost Jesus' blood to redeem me; now I live for His glory (I Corinthians 6:20).

God has given me the privilege to be part of His church (I Corinthians 12:27).

I have the privilege to come to God by His Spirit (Ephesians 2:18).

In Christ, I am complete (Colossians 1:14).

I know that all things work together for my good (Romans 8:28).

I am in Christ; therefore, Satan cannot cause me to fall (Colossians 3:3).

I do not live in fear, but I have power, love, and a sound mind (II Timothy 1:7).

I may come to God and find mercy and grace sufficient. (Hebrews 4:16).

When I find my sufficiency in Jesus, my life will bring forth fruit.

I will be a preserving element for family and friends (Matthew 5:13 & 16).

I will be willing to allow God to prune my life for greater usefulness (John 15:1-5).

I am called to be a witness at home, in the community, and abroad (Acts 1:8).

I am an ambassador for God to bring healing to others (II Corinthians 5:17-20).

I am worthy to be a joint-laborer with God (II Corinthians 6:1).

I can do all things through Jesus who strengthens me (Philippians 4:13).

God has given each person a talent or talents, and each needs to be diligent to use the talents to fulfill God's plan. It is not the ability that God judges, but faithfulness.

The account of Matthew 25 gives us the story of the ten talents. One person was given five talents, another two talents, and the third person was given one talent. When the master returned, he asked his servants to give an account of the talents he had distributed. The first had gained five more talents, the second had gained two more talents, but the third had buried his talent. The master was angry with the slothful servant and gave the buried talent to the one who already had ten talents. "For unto everyone that hath shall be given, and he shall have abundance: but from him that hath not shall be taken away even that which he hath" (verse 29). God always rewards faithfulness, and we must recognize we do not have time to envy or be jealous of others. God's will is to be busy seeking His favor and His approval, not to covet our neighbor's talents or abilities.

God expects us to be interested and concerned about other's well-being. Rather than resenting, we are to esteem others better than ourselves. "For I say to every man that is among you, not to think of himself more highly than he ought to think; but to think soberly." (Romans 12:3).

God wants us to rejoice with those who succeed rather than lament any misfortune or harbor jealousy.

It is not possible to work through such a trick of Satan alone, neither do we have to. Rather, we must confess the sin of jealousy and renounce it. "If we confess our sins, he is faithful and just to forgive our sins, and to cleanse us from all unrighteousness" (I John 1:9).

Jealousy, like the octopus, is truly a devil fish, and we dare not allow its tentacles to crush or entwine. Only by Jesus' blood, can it be rooted out and replaced by love.

Jealousy is not a respecter of persons, but it will grasp and imprison anyone within reach. It corrupts all people in some degree, at one time or another. But by Jesus' blood and His resurrecting power, all may be victorious.

"I can do all things through Christ which strengtheneth me" (Philippians 4:13). Then from a heart will come forth fruits of
> gratitude,
>> stability,
>>> humility,
>>>> joy,
>>>>> peace,
>>>>>> and security.

There will be no room left for the octopus of jealousy!

A Prayer for Holiness

Lord, may my life be pure and holy,
Free from all strife, humble and lowly;
A vessel fit for the Potter's use,
Help me to accept whate're You choose.

As You perfect me, O Lord, I pray,
May I be willing each passing day,
To say No to my fleshly desire,
Hearing You call me ever higher.

Though the world ever so loudly call,
And all around me many do fall,
Daily I'd walk in Your holy ways,
And Thine be all the glory and praise.

Though all my friends may turn against me,
May this ever be my humble plea,
Holier, higher, purer, I pray,
Lead me, O God, in Thy holy way.

– Mrs. Ruth Weaver
used by permission 1999

6

Just a Woman, or a Just Woman?

Every woman finds herself either as just a woman or a just woman. Faith in God is the ingredient that makes all the difference in her life.

It is interesting to notice the definition of *just*. The first definition for *just* is to engage in personal combat or competition." The second indicates "conforming to a standard of correctness, faithful to an original; righteous, fair, and upright."

The phrase, "The just shall live by faith," is found four times throughout the Bible (Habakkuk 2:4; Romans 1:17; Galatians 3:11; Hebrews 10:38). A proper reverence for God is the motivating factor in the person's life who lives by faith. That gives the woman a desire to be a just woman.

Faith is defined as "allegiance and loyalty to God, fidelity to ones promises." The Bible tells us that "faith is the substance (an ultimate reality that underlies all outward manifestation, Websters) of things hoped for, the evidence of things not seen" (Hebrews 11:1). Faith is the confidence that God is the Supreme Creator and Sustainer of the universe. It also gives us the assurance that He means what He says and He says what He means, and there is no guess work.

Isaiah 49:15 asks a question, "Can a mother forget her child?" It is not probable. Yet God said even though a mother would forget her child, yet He will not forget. Verse 16 tells us why – because He has graven us upon the palms of His hands. Perhaps this is where the cliche comes from, "Write it on your hand, so you don't forget."

There have possibly been times in every woman's life when she felt as though she was just a woman. We may have had a competitive spirit or even felt as if we needed to fight for our rights. I know I have, but by God's grace we do not need to live in such a state. I have allowed circumstances and people, words and attitudes, to dictate my life, and in doing so I stepped away from God.

The Greek root word for *just* is "to grow up, to exalt in triumph." In order to be a just woman and to have faith in God, we must be victorious over self and sin and continue to grow in the Christian life.

Hebrews 11 is often referred to as the faith chapter. The heroes of the Old Testament went through severe trials. But each managed to hold on to a trust in God despite the hardship. In doing so, their faith became more established in God, more fixed on the eternal purpose. Their faith could then enable them to transcend any trial or hardship. We desperately need this kind of faith in order to be just women in the twentieth century. In every circumstance of life God is glorified when we learn to see beyond the physical reality of this world to the spiritual. When we fail to see God as omnipotent, we often set ourselves up for a crashing disappointment. We live for the present rather than by faith. We forget that God has our lives in the palm of His hand.

In order to be just women we must develop a wholehearted commitment to God, apart from our circumstances.

The first step of faith for the just woman must be a broken, submissive, and teachable spirit (James 3:17). A broken object is open. So we must be open to receive instruction from God and others. "Except a corn of wheat fall into the ground and die, it abideth alone; but if it die, it bringeth forth much fruit" (John 12:24). Not until I deliberately sign away my rights to the Lordship of Jesus do I become a woman of faith.

Obedience is the second step to a life of faith. Obedience in all things. Obedience to all of God's commandments. Obedience that comes from the heart because we love God with all our heart, soul, and mind (Matthew 22:37). When we live in obedience, our steps will be ordered by the Lord (Psalm 37:23). Our words and actions will exemplify the Lord Jesus, and our daily lives will encourage others to live by faith.

The third step of faith is to stand for the truth. At times this may mean I need to stand alone. All of these radiant saints in Hebrews 11 needed to stand alone to be counted for God. Their faith was put to the test. Only as they were just men and women were they able to look beyond the present to the eternal and have the assurance that God knew what was happening to them.

John 21:15-22 gives us the account of Peter's reconciliation to Jesus after his denial. When Jesus asked Peter to follow him, his first response was so human; he was concerned about his fellow disciple John. But Jesus' reply was, "What is that to thee? follow thou me" (John 21:22b). God does not allow us to compare ourselves to others. Rather, God wants total allegiance.

Daniel is a good example of one whom God asked to stand alone (Daniel 1:8). He purposed in his heart not to defile himself. Daniel proved to be a just man and one whose character spoke of obedience and submission, even though he had to stand alone.

Joseph's life is recorded in Genesis 37-47. His life is another example of a just man who counted for God. All through Joseph's life he at times needed to stand alone. He was hated and envied by his brothers, who finally sold him to some merchants on their way to Egypt. He was falsely accused by Potiphar's wife and was sent to prison for a number of years. Never once did he blame God for his circumstances, but remained true to God by being obedient, submissive, and standing alone. In the latter years of Joseph's life, he was richly blessed by God.

Queen Esther was noted as a just woman who lived by faith. In Esther 4:16b she expressed her commitment, "If I perish, I perish." She had been an obedient and submissive young girl; therefore, God had a special work for her to do. She was willing to risk her life to bring her petition to the king, as it was unlawful to come before the king without being invited. Because Queen Esther was a just woman, she was willing to stand alone, and God honored her dedication by saving the whole Jewish nation.

God still honors those who meet His requirements and those who live by faith. Many times God blesses far beyond our expectations when we are willing to obey, submit, and stand for truth, even if it means to stand alone.

"The just [woman] shall live by faith" (Hebrews 10:38).

She will be aware that the path God chooses for her may be lonely, yet she knows God sees and cares.

Because of faith in God, while she may feel all alone, yet deep within her heart she knows God cares for the least of His children.

Because of faith in God, even though her prayers may seem unanswered, she is confident that God in His wisdom never forgets her.

Because of faith in God, she waits on the Lord, she trusts in His word, and she is patient and courageous.

Because of faith in God, she has a deep settled peace, even when burdened by grief and despair. Therefore she is able to cast all her cares upon God and leave them there.

Because of faith in God, she may need to pass through deep valleys, through the fire of adversity, over high, rough, and steep mountains, but she is able.

Because of faith in God, she has the assurance and confidence that God's love does not fail. Though all earthly kingdoms should perish, she knows God rules and reigns. She knows He is over all.

God cannot fail! He will not fail! Therefore we can each one be a just woman who lives by faith.

Being a just woman is not a special category of specially gifted or inspired people. It is the person whose heart is turned toward God, the one who knows her own righteousness does not count. Therefore she lives in God's righteousness.

Attributes of a Godly Woman

She is at peace with herself and God.

She is committed to God's headship order (I Cor. 11:1-16).

She has a meek and quiet spirit.

She has a servant heart.

She does not call attention to her physical beauty.

She considers homemaking a high and noble call.

She is a joyful person.

She is a woman of prayer and devotion to God.

She has learned the secret of Isaiah 26:3.

7

Peace, Perfect Peace

"Thou wilt keep [her] in perfect peace, whose mind is stayed on thee: because [she] trusteth in thee" (Isaiah 26:3).

Thank God for peace in a world of turmoil and chaos. Everyone desires peace. Many are searching for peace in the wrong places. Material gain, luxuries, vacations, fashionable lifestyles, and recreation are all pursued in search of peace and contentment.

The peace of God is not found in outward circumstances. It is a gift from God to the person who loves God and desires to please Him with all his heart. There are several steps that need to be taken in order to experience the wonderful peace of God.

The first step is to acknowledge that one is a sinner in need of a Savior. "For all have sinned, and come short of the glory of God" (Romans 3:23). He must ask Jesus to come into his heart and reign there. "That if thou shalt confess with thy mouth the Lord Jesus, and shalt believe in thine heart that God hath raised him from the dead, thou shalt be saved" (Romans 10:9).

Repentance is the second step in finding God's peace. To repent is to find victory over sin. It is to make a 180-degree turn and to say no to our selfish desires. Then the desire is to live wholly for Jesus as Savior and Lord.

Colossians 3:1-10 gives the procedure of repentance. We die to self and rise in Jesus' resurrecting power. We put off all the sins of the flesh and put on the new man which has been renewed by God.

The third step is to confess and make restitution. Proverbs 28:13 says, "He that covereth his sins shall not prosper: but whoso confesseth and forsaketh them shall have mercy." What a blessing to experience peace and joy! It is a clean feeling in the heart that cannot be explained by words. This is peace!

F. B. Meyers, in his book, *Great Verses Through the Bible*, so aptly writes, "The Hebrew is very significant. Perfect peace means peace, peace. It is, as it were, the soul dwelling between double doors. If one assurance isn't enough, God will follow with the second and even the third peace if necessary." It is God's plan for His children to enjoy peace of heart and mind, peace with God and oneself. It is also His will that we "follow peace with all men . . ." (Hebrews 12:14).

Peace, God's peace, affects our everyday living. It is not for a season; it is a way of life. All four Gospels record that. Jesus brought peace in the midst of a storm (Matthew 14:22-31; Mark 6:45-51; Luke 8:22-25; John 6:16:21). And so it is yet today. If we have met the conditions set forth in God's Word, we can also be assured that when Jesus reigns in our hearts, we too can enjoy peace and calm, even in the midst of a severe storm.

Many times we have ample opportunity in our homes to exercise a peaceful attitude.

A young, expectant mother wakes during the night and fear grips her heart. What if the baby will come early? What if . . . ?

A small toddler experiences a hard fall and the mother

is fearful; what if he has head injuries?

A mother is overwhelmed by the sensitivity of her four-year-old. The child fears so much that she is unable to sleep at night.

A mother of school children has concerns about her children. The telephone rings at 3:15 PM and she just knows it's his teacher with a complaint.

A youth girl enjoys her job so much, and all at once she loses her job. The future looms like a black cloud. What does God have in store for her?

A young man is searching to know God's will, and there are obstacles that seem to block his knowing God's will.

A pastor's wife has a full schedule, and yet there are needs that seemingly go unmet. There is a sorrowing neighbor whose husband fell over dead; food and comfort should be brought to them. A telephone conversation indicates a very discouraged person. Another call jolts the pastor's wife that it is a blessing to be able to work. "If only I could work" comes from the voice at the other end of the line.

In all the experiences listed, there are two ways one can respond. One can respond in frustration, develop a headache, and perhaps hurt someone by harsh words. Or one can respond in the calm assurance of God's wonderful peace and draw from His resources. "And let the peace of God rule in your hearts, to the which also ye are called . . . and be ye thankful" (Colossians 3:15). When the peace of God rules, it may not change the circumstances or take the pressure away, but we can cast our care on him; "for he careth for [us]" (I Peter 5:7).

Many of us like a schedule and perhaps go to great lengths to plan our work. But when the peace of God rules the heart, we will pray that we can be flexible and follow His plan instead of asking God to bless our plans.

Satan is out to undermine, and he loves to destroy the peace God wants to impart to His children. When the young mother woke up during the night and fear gripped her heart, it was Satan trying to destroy her peace. Whenever a person seeks God with all his heart, Satan is there to try to frustrate, confuse, and overwhelm. He doesn't care how, just so he can work against God. Satan is mean enough to tempt a person in an area that he is unable to change.

Peace is a gift from God, and it strengthens faith in God. When we have peace with God and are at peace within our hearts, we know God is all-sufficient. Then we are able to trust Him completely in all life's details.

Yes, God keeps us in perfect peace when our mind dwells on Him, because then we can trust God fully.

A godly
perspective
makes all the
difference in
the world.

Let Not Your Heart Be Troubled

Let not your heart be troubled,
Just believe in me.
I have gone to prepare,
A heavenly place for thee.

Do not be afraid,
I know each step you take,
I'll ever be at your side,
And never you forsake.

Let not your heart be troubled,
I will come again for you,
To take you where I am,
So you can be there too.

Do not be afraid,
In this world of sin and strife.
Believe in me for I am
The way, the truth, the life.

Miriam Chupp
used by permission, 1999

8

With Jesus in the Storm

Many people are afraid of thunderstorms, I have been no exception. And I have not passed calmness through a storm on to my children as much as I have desired to.

Some parents, when they notice a storm is brewing, will quickly gather the family into the house and sit quietly in the living room or go to an underground basement or cellar. If a storm advances during the night, they waken the family and get dressed in case evacuation is necessary.

In another home, the four children would all congregate in their parents' bed. They were awakened by the first crash of thunder, and they felt more secure close to their parents. One child was comforted by the song, "Til the Storm Passes Over."

One father would go to the door and watch the approaching storm. As his son grew older, he would stand beside his father and together they would view God's marvelous handiwork. The father would point out various formations of clouds and different streaks of lightning. This boy grew up to enjoy thunderstorms.

A veteran missionary was visiting when her hosts noticed a storm was fast approaching. The command was given to run to the basement. Rather than run, she chose to watch the formation of the storm. She felt no fear as she said, "If Jesus comes, I'm ready." Instead of running, she was awed by God's greatness.

Songs express the thought that life is a voyage and is sometimes referred to as a ship at sea. Phrases such as "Jesus the Captain," "Jesus, pilot me," and "Jesus at the helm" all give the word pictures of Jesus and the storm.

The Bible gives numerous accounts of storms. The four Gospel writers must have been intrigued with the account of Jesus and the storm (Matthew 14:22-31; Mark 4:35-41; Luke 8:22-25; John 6:16-21). All four were inspired to include it, and to be sure, it must have been marvelous to have Jesus calm the wind and waves by His spoken word. Jesus still speaks peace in the midst of a gathering storm, even if it is a spiritual storm that we encounter.

The account in Mark was impressive to me even as a child. Imagine Jesus right in your boat asleep on a pillow (v. 38). His very presence brought security, especially as the winds started to rock the boat and the waves splashed higher and higher. The disciples were alert. They noticed the stars were disappearing and the moon no longer shone. A glance toward Jesus told them He was unafraid, and His very presence brought hope and peace to their troubled hearts.

Conveying a calm and peaceful spirit to our children in the midst of a storm is no easy task. As Christians we have the promise that Jesus is omnipresent and omniscient. We face many trying times in life, and these can be referred to as storms that threaten to wreck our ship at sea. Only as we have a vibrant relationship with the heavenly Father can we experience the calm, whether we are facing a storm or living in the sunshine of life. As we follow God's principles, we can be assured we will be kept in perfect peace as our minds are stayed on Him (Isaiah 26:3).

Husbands and wives have different ideas and different ways of doing the same things. Unless Jesus has control of our hearts and has transformed our hearts by His grace, we may encounter furious storms. Self must be brought to Calvary in both partners' lives; then we can safely face the storm that threatens shipwreck. It is God's design that each storm is approached by His grace. Together we are better prepared to serve Him and to complement each other.

"The fear of man bringeth a snare: but whoso putteth his trust in the Lord shall be safe" (Proverbs 29:25). Many times it is the little differences that wreck a marriage – little inconsistencies, little discourtesies, little words that hurt, and little disrespects. In many of these areas we choose whether we will allow Jesus to bring peace and a love that understands, or whether self is permitted to cause problems. Perhaps husband and wife have come to an agreement on how to squeeze the tooth paste tube. For a short time it is done as agreed upon but, then at an unguarded moment, one squeezes the middle of the tube. This can become a source of irritation in the subconscious mind.

We may be polite and courteous to each other most of the time, but it must become our way of life lest at a tense moment one becomes very rude. One angry or hurtful word can cut deep into the soul and wound the spirit of the partner. It may take many kind words, asking for forgiveness, and a sincere proving to regain confidence.

All family members may know where to find their clothes. They may even be arranged to the extent that one can open a drawer and find the right clothes at the right place in the dark. But one little inconsistency can destroy that blessing.

Car keys need to be placed in the appointed place so everyone will know where to find them. Our family of six was used to all having their own set of keys. When we purchased our last car, we discovered it was costly to each have a set, so we needed to change our system. It works well as long as we are all concerned about keeping our side of the agreement. It has proven a good experience to adjust to a different way of handling a very small issue. The secret is in consistency.

Carelessness is often at the beginning of a storm that threatens shipwreck.

Choosing our reading material can result in a conflict that causes a storm, unless we seek God's direction first. *The Daily News*, *Reader's Digest*, and *Enquire* provide food for the flesh and can be a detriment to one's spiritual appetite. Filling our minds with other people's sins tends to dull us to the exceeding sinfulness of sin in God's sight. Many people hide behind the cloak of being concerned about world affairs and wanting to be aware of what's happening so that they can help people, when actually deep in their hearts they are finding sensual pleasure in reading about other's wrong doings. God not only condemns sin, but also those who take pleasure in it. What we feed on is what we become. "As [a person] thinketh in his heart, so is he" (Proverbs 23:7).

During the time I was writing this chapter, it seemed Satan brought a number of trials and differences into our lives to try to undermine and destroy. I was challenged anew that claiming the blood of Jesus is one thing Satan cannot touch. Only as couples and families live by God's principles is there victory. And only then are we able to stand against the wiles of the devil. We must be strong in God's strength and in His might, and put on the whole armor of God in order to stand (Ephesians 6:10, 11).

Numerous times in the Apostle Paul's writings, he

shows the contrast between the flesh and the Spirit. The flesh is at the center of wrong desires and selfish ambitions, and thus of sin and all its consequences. Following the flesh, minding the flesh, or desiring selfish impulses leads to storms that end in shipwreck, because the flesh leads to a darkened mind and a dulled conscience. Misery, bondage, despair, quarreling, frustration, hatred, bitterness, depression, and gloom are all associated with the works and ways of the flesh. Therefore Jesus is not present to calm the storm.

The Spirit of God stands in direct opposition to the flesh and to all its thinking and ways. When a person opens his heart to Jesus as Savior and Lord of his life, and the Holy Spirit takes up residence there, there will be holy war declared on the flesh.

There can be no bargaining and compromise. God's Word is forever settled in heaven (Psalm 119:89). God's Word "is true from the beginning" (Psalm 119:160). And God's Word is the same "yesterday, today, and forever" (Hebrews 13:8). If one doubts these verses, he should read Malachi 3:6: "For I am the Lord, I change not." "The carnal mind is enmity against God; for it is not subject to the law of God, neither indeed can be. So then they that are in the flesh cannot please God" (Romans 8:7, 8).

In order to face the storms of life successfully and victoriously, we must be filled with the Holy Spirit. To be spiritually minded, to walk in the Spirit, requires that we "mortify" the flesh, that is, put it to death and render it powerless.

When we do this, the Holy Spirit is free to do His work in us. His work reproduces the likeness of Jesus in our words, attitudes, and actions. Paul refers to this as the fruit of the Spirit (Galatians 5:22).

It is sad but true that many people want the benefits of the indwelling Spirit (a deep satisfaction and boundless joy), while still clinging to attitudes and actions motivated by the flesh.

When the Holy Spirit has His way in the hearts of people, the evidence is not primarily what such a person can do, but rather what he becomes.

He is characterized by:

LOVE: a sacrificial commitment to the good of others.

JOY: an overflowing spirit of gratitude and praise focused on the unmerited grace of God.

PEACE: an inner calm that results from a cleansed heart and a restored relationship with God.

LONGSUFFERING: a willingness to bear with difficult people while helping them God-ward.

GENTLENESS: a kind sensitivity toward the feelings and needs of others.

GOODNESS: freedom from guile and hypocrisy.

FAITH: an absolute trust in God and a certainty that His will for my life is best.

MEEKNESS: a gentle, humble manner in responding to any annoyance.

TEMPERANCE: an inner strength to keep all appetites and affections in proper bounds.

These qualities form the fruit of the Spirit, the day-by-day evidence that the flesh has been rendered inoperative and the Holy Spirit of God has taken up permanent residence.

A. W. Tozer so aptly wrote, "When we surrender ourselves to God's meekness, we will not care what people will think of us, as long as God is pleased. Then what we are will be everything; what we appear will take its place far down the scale of interest for us. Apart from sin we have nothing of which to be ashamed."

The ship at sea, where Jesus is present, is more than mere sentiment, and the trials are more than mere dreaming. All members are real humans with their shortcomings and possibilities. Everyone has problems that need to be solved, real duties to perform, and real difficulties to overcome. And these will be resolved only as they are worked out in the heaven-approved way.

"Blessed are the pure in heart: for they shall see God [in everything]" (Matthew 5:8). We can have the confidence that any family can brave the storms we encounter in life (and come through more mature and better prepared to serve our Lord and Savior) as we meet the conditions set forth in God's Word. We can, by His grace, watch as the storm approaches and see the wonderful way God leads His children, because Jesus is in the storm and speaks, "Peace be still."

My Pacesetter

The Lord is my pacesetter, I shall not rush.

He makes me to stop for quiet intervals.
He provides me with images of stillness which restore my serenity.

He leads me in ways of efficiency through calmness of mind,
and His guidance is peace.

Even though I have a great many things to accomplish each day,
I will not fret, for His presence is here.
His timelessness, His all-importance will keep me in balance.

He prepares refreshment in the midst of my activity
by anointing my mind with his oil of tranquility.
My cup of joyous energy overflows.

Surely harmony and effectiveness shall be the fruit of my hours,
and I shall walk in the pace of the Lord
and dwell in His house forever.

                                        -- Author Unknown

9

Is It Beth-el or El-Beth-el?

It was a sad day when Jacob was asked to leave his home, his mother whom he loved, his father whom he had deceived, and his twin brother who hated him. This account is found in Genesis 27. In verse 43, we read that Rebecca, Jacob's mother, noticed the hatred in Esau and advised her favorite son not only to leave home, but to flee for his life.

I cannot imagine the overwhelming feeling that engulfed Jacob's heart as he quickly packed a few belongings, just what he could easily carry on his shoulder. Perhaps he looked back long enough for his eyes to overflow with tears, or maybe the urgency was so great that he dared not lose a moment of time, but ran as fast as he could.

His mother had advised him to return to her family in Padan-aram, which was approximately five hundred miles north of Gerar where Jacob lived with his father, mother, and twin brother. His journey included two hundred miles of desert travel. In Genesis 28, vv 10-15, we read that the journey was very lonely. He must have traveled between forty to fifty miles the first day. As darkness fell, he was extremely weary. He was alone, all alone, away from everything that was familiar, with no place to resort to. The heavens were his only canopy and curtains. A stone offered his tired head a place of rest. God and the angels were his only hope and protection.

In his hard lodging he had a sweet dream. He saw a ladder which reached from earth to heaven, with God at the top, and angels ascending and descending upon it. This dream gave Jacob comfort, informing him that God was guiding and protecting his life. Jacob was apprehensive of danger from his brother Esau, but now he had the assurance that God would bless his long journey.

In the morning Jacob felt blessed and refreshed because God had revealed Himself through a vision. Jacob in gratitude poured oil on the stone that had pillowed his head and called the place Beth-el. In Hebrew *Beth-el* means "the house of God." Verse 16 says, "And Jacob awaked out of his sleep, and he said, 'Surely the Lord is in this place; and I knew it not.'" God encouraged him in verse 15, "And, behold, I am with thee, and will keep thee . . . I will not leave thee." What a wonderful promise to dwell on the rest of his journey.

Have you ever experienced being forsaken by friends or family? Perhaps you have felt as if you had nowhere to turn, until you had encouragement from a Bible passage or a kind word from an angel unaware. Then you woke up to the realization that God was in this situation and you weren't aware of it. This becomes your Beth-el.

God does not want us to stay in this situation, and just as he promised Jacob, He won't leave us either. God has a plan for each life. With the encouragement of Beth-el, where God meets us, we can go on through the desert of our lives and be able to come through victoriously. There is no place that precludes divine visits.

In Genesis 29, we read that Jacob reached his destination safely and enjoyed God's blessings. By divine providence, he was led to his uncle's family. In the process of time, God blessed Jacob with a family and much cattle.

After more than twenty years of hard work for his father-in-law, God instructed Jacob to return to his homeland. This time he was not to go alone, but with a great company of people and cattle (Genesis 32).

Jacob's first memorable encounter with God was on his way to Padan-aram. On his way back he met God again. It wasn't until after he suffered injustice and wrestled with an angel that Jacob recalled his first encounter with God. He changed the name of Beth-el to El-Beth-el. Jacob shifted his emphasis from the sacred place of God to the Supreme God he had now met face to face (Genesis 35:7). Finally, God took the central place in his life.

It is God's design for us today, too, to meet God face to face and serve the Supreme God (El-Beth-el) of the House of God (Beth-el). God's will is for His children to know Him. He desires us to grow from the first encounter of meeting God to our total focus on the Supreme God of the universe. "And this is life eternal, that they might know thee the only true God, and Jesus Christ, whom thou has sent" (John 17:3).

In the three epistles of John we read the phrase "we know" twenty-seven times. It was of utmost importance to the writer that people learn to know God. To know Him personally is much more than just knowing about Him. Jacob in his first encounter was amazed and wondered that God was in that place. Years later he shifted his focus from the amazement of God's presence to the reality that He is God of the House of God. It was God who now captured his attention.

God allows us to go through trying and difficult experiences to enable us to get a glimpse of His holiness and greatness. Knowing God and growing in this knowledge develops in us the blessed assurance that we can trust God more fully, and then even more fully. As we grow in knowing God, we come to realize that the safest place to be is in God's will. We then turn from what we want to do to seek to know God's plan for us. We grow in knowledge of God's will by seeking Him with all our hearts. "Seek the LORD and his strength, seek his face continually" (I Chronicles 16:11).

As we experience the assurance that we are submitted to God's will, we have a peace of heart and mind that fortifies us against the tactics and temptations that Satan uses to undermine God's work. Being assured of God's stamp of approval on one's life gives him the confidence he needs to go on trusting God more fully. Assurance and confidence in God equips us with a sense of accomplishment and gives us purpose for living. That brings us fullness of joy.

When I believe in God's salvation, trust in His goodness, and appropriate the grace of God in my everyday life, my goal is clear because I have complete confidence and trust in my Master. Many people never get beyond Beth-el. God is in their thoughts, but He is not given first place. Always, God must be first!

Is it Beth-el or El-Beth-el? The choice is ours!

Our greatest
opportunity
is to make an
eternal difference.

My Influence

My life shall touch a dozen lives
Before this day is done;
Leave countless marks for good or ill,
Ere sets the evening sun.

So this the wish I always wish,
The prayer I ever pray
"Lord, may my life help other lives
It touches by the way."

—copied
Pulpit Helps
published by AMG Publishers
Chattanooga, TN 27422

10
The Power of Influence

To my amazement, as I looked out my kitchen window, I saw three small fawns gingerly approaching the border of the woods. They curiously began nibbling the grass. When this occurred every morning, it became obvious they were orphans and had no mother to alert them of danger. As we watched them, they would look and then aimlessly trot out of sight.

Several weeks later on an early Sunday morning walk, I saw another fawn and by its side was a very prudent mother. In a moment her tail swayed and with a snort she gracefully bounded into the woods. The fawn followed her example. What a paradigm!

As I continued to observe the three orphans, my heart ached and tears came to my eyes as I deliberated on the fact that there are many children and adults who are orphaned from a good influence and example to follow. Many just trot aimlessly through life without someone to point them to Jesus, and to a solid and wholesome way of life.

Influence is described by Webster as the power exerted over the mind and behavior of others. It inevitably influences for weal or woe.

According to the Bible it does not matter whether or not we were born in a Christian home. Paul tells us in Romans

5:19, "For by one man's disobedience [failing to hear, heed-lessness and carelessness] many [for all] were made sinners, so by the obedience of one [Jesus] shall many be made righteous." Adam and Eve disobeyed God by eating of the forbidden fruit (see Genesis 3:1-24). They influenced all people to sin, but Jesus the perfect Son of God also influences people to follow the example of His obedience to His Father. "Though he were a Son, yet learned he obedience by the things which he suffered" (Hebrews 5:8; also read Philippians 2:5-8).

We have all been created by God to follow someone. God is the only original One; no other person is original. We have only rearranged our pattern of thinking by someone who has achieved. An architect was once asked how much of his work was original with him. He replied, "Only five percent." Could it be safe to say that influence is ninety-five percent of an individual? Then a godly influence is imperative!

In Ephesians 5:1 Paul instructs, "Be ye therefore followers of God as dear children." The Amplified version states it clearer, "Therefore be imitators of God [copy Him and follow His example] as well-beloved children [imitate their father]."

Children are indeed imitators. What an overwhelming responsibility to imitate our Father God so closely that we can be an influential example to our children!

Influence in everyday life can often be exemplified in the spiritual life as well. Little children are seen playing in the snow, trying to follow in their daddy's large footsteps and saying, "Daddy, I'm following you." A little three-year-old son was "helping" his mother do the dishes, and he admiringly told her, "When I'm big, I want to be a mommy just like you." A young four-year-old, while his daddy was giving him a hair cut, said, "I want a hair cut like Bennie." (He is bald.)

How very important to represent God properly to our children! How awesome to be an example for others to follow! Example, influence—what a far-reaching effect it has for God or the devil!

I could not have been more than five years old, but the memory returns to me yet with vivid freshness. One of my favorite preachers would preach with such fervor. He would often speak directly to the children. His illustrations were so easy to follow. I just loved him. In my childish mind I thought once I'm his age, I'll know all there is to know. To me, he knew God so intimately, so reverently, that his daily life spoke volumes. Years have glided by and he has long ago entered his rest, but his meek, gentle, and humble manner of living has left its imprint on me. His influence has left an indelible impression on my life. He was a living example of one who sincerely imitated God. He copied and followed God's pattern.

Paul, in all of his writings, always pointed people to God. "Be ye followers of me, even as I also am of Christ" (I Corinthians 11:1). We have many examples of people who followed God closely, and their lives still speak today. Hebrews 11 records forty verses of people of influence. Throughout the chapter faith is the key. "But without faith it is impossible to please [God]; for he that cometh to God must believe that he is, and that he is a rewarder of them that diligently seek Him" (v. 6).

In order to be a person that follows God, one that is a godly influence, the first ingredient is faith in God and in His Word. Since God's Word is "forever...settled in heaven" (Psalm 119:89), we can depend on it. His Word is a road map to show us clearly how to live. We also have the promise that by seeking God and following Him, He will take care of our needs. "But seek ye first the kingdom of God, and His righteousness: and all these things shall be added unto you" (Matthew 6: 33). "But my God shall supply all your need according to his riches in glory by Christ Jesus" (Philippians 4:19).

God has provided the Holy Spirit to guide us into all truth. "When the Spirit of truth, is come, he will guide you into all truth" (John 16:13). To be a good influence, it is imperative to have a sensitive spirit, one that is pliable and useful in God's service and sensitive to His still small voice. There will be times when God will change our priorities from earthly to heavenly goals.

We can trust Jesus to lead us safely. When we choose our destiny, we accept God's route; but if we in our selfish pursuits choose the route, then we will need to accept the destiny.

Faith comes by hearing and hearing by the Word of God (Romans 10:17). Listening and really hearing is an art. We must train ourselves to listen and hear. We either tune our ears to hear or not to hear.

In Matthew 9:9, we read of the influence Jesus had when he called Matthew to be his disciple. Jesus said, "Follow me." Matthew arose and followed him. Jesus' call took priority. Jesus called and Matthew responded NOW.

The challenge of influence now rests on us. Should some soul be silently tracking my life, what impact do I leave? God grant me the grace and power to be a positive influence on others.

Knowing and loving
God is the foundation
upon which everything
else rests.

As a woman from God's perspective,
God desires that we
Christ
Has
Assurance
aNd
Grace
Enough
into His likeness.
He gives

Wisdom – *the ability to look at life from God's perspective.*

Insight – *the ability to see through each situation from God's perspective.*

Understanding – *the ability to respond to life from God's perspective.*

11
Two Things Lacking

When we look at the increasing loneliness, inner anguish, hunger, violence, and war in this world, we know for a certainty that the powers of darkness are very active among us. As Christians, we should have courage to face these powers in the conviction that our Lord has overcome them through His death and resurrection. Nevertheless, in this world many lack the assurance and security (two things lacking) that every child of God can know through a vital relationship with the Good Shepherd.

It seems the circumstances in which we live could not get worse. In Genesis 6:5, we read, ". . . that every imagination of the thoughts of his heart was only evil continually." The world had become so sinful that God regretted He had created man. Verse 6 reads, "And it repented the Lord that he had made man on the earth, and it grieved him at his heart."

The scene changes in verses 8 and 9. "But Noah found grace in the eyes of the Lord...Noah was a just man and perfect in his generations, and Noah walked with God." God was pleased with Noah. God had a plan and in His plan Noah would be an instrument God could use to bring assurance and security to all who would obey. Noah and his wife, their three sons and their wives, would be safe in the ark, while God destroyed all of the earth's wickedness (read Genesis 7:23.)

There is still an ark of protection available for all who take God's Word seriously (read I Peter 3:20, 21.) It's the precious blood of Jesus. That is one thing Satan cannot touch. For that reason, it is so important that our sins are confessed and our lives cleansed by Jesus' blood. Then within this realm we have assurance and security. There is a dimension of freedom that is known in no other way. It is the freedom to become all God has planned for us to become.

Since it is a choice, it becomes our responsibility to comply and conform to God's will. Then Psalm 23 will be a comfort and guide for our life.

Either we choose the destiny and accept God's way or we take our own way and accept the destiny. But when we choose the destiny and leave our way to God's all-wise plan, we will know assuredly that "the LORD [indeed] is my shepherd." We have the confidence, then, that whatever He brings into our lives has already passed the approval of the Good Shepherd. He has permitted that experience for our eternal good.

God has a good reason for comparing His people to sheep. Of all of God's creation, sheep are the most likely to get lost. We have all heard of animals that finally found their way back to their original owners, but not so with a sheep. A sheep becomes disoriented and someone must search for it (read Luke 15:3-7).

As people, we are unable to save ourselves. God sent Jesus, His Son, to give His life for us. He searched and found us when we were unlovely. Jesus brought the plan of salvation, the way to victory; therefore, knowing the Shepherd is security.

"I shall not want," is a complete statement, as well as self-explanatory. I shall have no need that Jesus cannot meet. "My God shall supply all your need according to his riches in glory by Christ Jesus " (Philippians 4:19). At times, we may get our wants and needs mixed up. Having the Good Shepherd to guide us, we shall not lack any good thing. "The LORD will give grace and glory: no good thing will he withhold from them that walk uprightly" (Psalm 84:11).

We find ourselves living in a society of rush and scurry, with little time to sit and meditate. "I shall not want" is not native to that kind of life style. It is a state of contentment that must be developed. And only as we learn to allow Him "to make [us] to lie down in green pastures," will we be nourished and become the recipients of God's loving care, finding our rest in Him.

Frequently, we like sheep wander outside the Shepherd's loving care, curiously exploring the forbidden. The Shepherd knows that in order for His sheep to be healthy, they must be refreshed by resting, by meditating, assimilating, and thoughtfully comprehending His greatness and wonders.

It takes time to be holy! God may at times put us on our backs in order to get our attention. Don't make the Shepherd take such strong measures; instead, spend time alone with Jesus. It will cause you to love the Shepherd more fervently.

The Good Shepherd leads His sheep "beside the still waters." Sheep are timid and gentle and need a quiet, refreshing stream to drink from. We, too, need the quiet refreshing, cool pools of spiritual refreshment. If we fail to drink from His still waters, we will not be equipped to face the spiritual tests that are sure to come.

Psalm 46:10 reminds us, "Be still, and know that I am God." God does not scream and shout to get our attention. He silently and quietly reveals His way to those who have time to listen and are sensitive to His still small voice.

Often we are so busy and hurried that we fail to receive clear direction from God. Indeed we are blessed when we pause momentarily and catch a glimpse of God's holiness and greatness. It truly is spiritually refreshing!

"He restoreth my soul: he leadeth me in the paths of righteousness for his name's sake." The ardent picture of the Good Shepherd and His sheep come to my mind. In His arms He is carrying a lamb, and the rest of the sheep follow closely, especially the lamb's mother. She looks up into the Shepherd's face, and He reaches out His hand and strokes her head. Sheep want to be loved. They are assured of His love and find real security in following their leader closely. We, too, should humbly praise and adore our Shepherd for His love and kindness to us.

"Yea, though I walk through the valley of the shadow of death, I will fear no evil; for thou art with me; thy rod and thy staff they comfort me." The same picture is portrayed again, the Good Shepherd leading His sheep through the narrow valley. On both sides are high and dangerous mountains. Wild animals lurk in crevices or ravines, ready to pounce on any sheep that lags behind.

Only as we stay close to the Shepherd are we kept from dangers that allure. His rod and staff may be used to guide us back to Himself.

"Thou preparest a table before me in the presence of mine enemies." The shepherd, while he fed his sheep, was careful that no poisonous snakes, insects, or weeds could harm them. So the Good Shepherd went to Calvary and took away the dread and fear of death, the last enemy (I

Corinthians 15:26).

We will all face death, but as we follow the Shepherd, we have the assurance that our sins are forgiven, and we have the security that nothing can separate us from God's great love (read Romans 8:32-39).

"Surely goodness and mercy shall follow me all the days of my life: and I will dwell in the house of the Lord forever." At the close of the day, when the shepherd would lead his sheep into the fold, he would pour oil in a wound or sore that had developed during the day. He noticed the one that limped or the one that lagged behind. He could detect if one was sick, and he ministered individually to each need. The Good Shepherd, Jesus, is concerned about every hurt or bruise that His children experience.

At the end of our journey, Jesus, the One who goes with us through the valley of the shadow of death, guides us safely to our eternal home.

It is truly His goodness and His unfailing mercy that protect, all the days of our life. Since our Shepherd is omnipresent, omnipotent, and omniscient, where could we find greater assurance and security?

We are absolutely secure in this blessed assurance!

Psalm 8

O Lord our Lord, how excellent Thy name in all the earth!
Let men give praise and honor from the moment of their birth!
For Thou hast set Thy glory high above the highest heav'n;
Let every creature praise Thy name, as long as breath be giv'n!
When I behold the heavens, which Thy finger hath arranged:
The sun, the planets, moon, and stars, their orbits all unchanged,
What can I do, a puny man, but lift my voice in praise,
And dedicate my life to Thee, to walk in all They ways?
For what I man, a speck of dust, that Thou should'st visit him?
Thou Who eternity hast spanned, and time is but a whim!
Yet man Thou has created just below th' angelic band
To have dominion over all upon the sea and land.
All cattle, sheep, and oxen, and the beast upon the field;
The fishes, birds, and creeping things, to man their power yield.
To have such great authority, I cannot understand;
Especially when I think of Thee, and of Thy mighty hand.
O Lord our Lord, in all the earth, how excellent Thy name!
Let every creature, everywhere, exalt and praise the same.

Enos Stutzman
Used by permission 1998

12

Why Take Side Trips?

Life is a journey through time to eternity. The journey that God has called His children to travel is always an upward climb (see Ecclesiastes 3:21). So, why take side trips? They take us away from God and always leads us downward. "Mine iniquities have taken hold upon me, so that I am not able to look up;" (Psalm 40:12). This verse indicates that it is sin and self that keeps us from stepping toward God.

Abraham was called the Friend of God (James 2:23), even though he did not always consult God. In Genesis 12 God called Abraham to leave his country, and he obeyed. In the course of time Abraham built an altar and called upon God for direction and blessing.

Abraham had no evil intentions when he went to Egypt, but rather than trusting God to provide during the famine, he took things into his own hands. While in Egypt, he became fearful that the king might take Sarah his beautiful wife for himself, so he instructed Sarah to lie about their relationship in order to save his life. Human reasoning is dangerous and often takes a person on side trips.

Noah is another example. In Genesis 9:18-28, we have the account of Noah's occupation after the Flood. He plant-ed a vineyard, and in the course of time he became drunk.

This was a side trip that left a blot on his name.

King David, though blessed by God, took side trips on several occasions. II Samuel 11 calls attention to David's idleness. He should have been the captain of his army, but instead he allowed his passions to control him, and finally, he committed adultery with Bathsheba.

It takes clear thinking to stay in tune with God. Idleness, on the contrary, is the devil's workshop. So thinking is an attribute of a busy person.

Samson is another example of one who allowed self to dictate his life, and he took side trips (Judges 14-16). He even ended his life because he was defeated by his passion.

Jonah rejected God's commands to go to Nineveh to preach (Jonah 1-4). After spending three days and nights in the whale's belly, he did go and preach. But rather than rejoicing when the people repented, he complained to God. Jonah enjoyed the side trips more than obeying God and rejoicing when God answered prayers.

If we as women think it is only the men of the Bible who took side trips, we are mistaken. Eve took a side trip unaccompanied by her husband. In Genesis 3, we read that God created Adam and Eve and placed them in a beautiful garden. It was a perfect paradise. Adam was a perfect husband and Eve was a perfect, beautiful wife. They had perfect fellowship with God. They were laborers together with God to care for their pleasant home. Everything was immaculate. We say Eve was a foolish woman. She took a side trip, listening to the serpent and eating of the forbidden fruit, even though they had all their hearts could desire.

We may be quick to judge Adam and Eve and say we would never do such a thing, not if we would have all the blessings Eve enjoyed. But wait a minute! How many times are we just as foolish as Eve? We, too, have been created by God. He has a perfect plan for each one of us. He has created a beautiful earth on which to live and glorify Him. God has given us the ability to choose the best of God's blessings. He has given us salvation through Jesus. We are truly rich in Him! We have the guidance of the Holy Spirit. We can live by His grace and live above the adverse circumstances of life. We can enjoy victory in Jesus because He lives in our hearts. By God's grace we can be channels for God's love to flow through to others. And best of all, we can have the assurance of eternal life. "And this is life eternal, that they might know thee the only true God, and Jesus Christ, whom thou hast sent" (John 17:3).

Instead of focusing on God, we, like Eve, take side trips! We become overwhelmed with the concerns and cares of rearing our families for God in the midst of a wicked world. Let us remember "When my heart is overwhelmed: lead me to the rock that is higher than I" (Psalm 61:2).

We may become discontented with our lot in life and think God is not fair. Instead of taking a side trip into depression and discouragement, let us remember, "In the morning will I direct my prayer unto thee, and will look up" (Psalm 5:3b).

As a young bride or expectant mother, the world may seem like a huge uncaring place in which to live as a couple and to bring children into the world. Let us remember, "The Lord is my shepherd; I shall not want" (Psalm 23:1).

As mothers of school-age children, we may become anxious as we see our children reaching out and learning from others. At times all the work may seem like a never-ending job. "What hast thou that thou didst not receive?" (I Corinthians 4:7). With every responsibility, there is grace sufficient as we seek God through His Word and prayer.

II Chronicles 25:9b encourages us: "The LORD is able to give thee much more than this." His grace and wisdom always supersedes our needs.

We may find ourselves growing older, and as our children leave home, they no longer need our constant care and guidance. Instead of a side trip into loneliness, let us remember: "When I am old and greyheaded, O God, forsake me not; until I have shewed thy strength unto this generation" (Psalm 71:18a). When we feel the tug of the side trip of loneliness, we need to read God's Word and pray for our families. There is always much to be done for the woman who is willing to allow God to use her. Life centers around the heart, therefore; we must "Keep [our] heart with all diligence; for out of it are the issues of life" (Proverbs 4:23).

Since the heart is the key to side trips, we must be diligent to keep our heart with all diligence. Then holy thoughts, kind feelings, and pure purposes will flow from there. A well-guarded heart provides the source of a well-regulated life of virtue, peacefulness, and sobriety. When we keep our heart with all diligence, it will ensure God's blessings, proper esteem, and joyful living.

"With God in control of our hearts, it will affect our mouth and lips. 'Put away from thee a froward mouth, and perverse lips put far from thee' (Proverbs 4:24). In controlling the mouth we are controlling the heart. Its contents must be purified from falsehood, coarseness, foolish talking, and gossip. Our eyes are to be trained to a direct and straightforward expression. 'Let thine eyes look right on, and let thine eyelids look straight before thee' (v. 25). Clear, honest light beams from the eyes of the pure and open-hearted. Eyes not only mirror the heart, but remind us how the heart may be reached by self-discipline of the eyes.

'Ponder the path of thy feet and let all thy ways be established' (v. 26). As the eyes so the feet are to be trained to a straightforward walk, even in moments of relaxation. Our mind needs direction and self-discipline; otherwise it becomes dissolute and lax." (Excerpt from *Pulpit Commentary*).

Keep your heart with all diligence is the key to side trips. God has a perfect plan for every woman. In His perfect plan is perfect peace to do His perfect will.

Victory at Dawn

Our God knows why there's darkened sky,
Unending night and wary fight.
He has a plan for ravaged man
When sad heart yearns and passion burns.
He will not leave me long to grieve
Hopes unfulfilled and dreams all stilled.
He'll answer soon, His way make known;
He'll make it clear, I need not fear.
Then morning comes, the darkness dims,
I'll say, "O light! I love thy sight!"
How could I think, while at dawn's brink,
So awful night, so long the fight!
I'm now made strong, and sing the song
Of patience's story, love's victory.

Mrs. Ruth Weaver
used by permission 1999

13
Contrary Winds

It was about 6:00 p.m. and Jesus had just served over five thousand people out on the mountainside. A little lad had been willing to share his lunch of five loaves of bread and two fish. The disciples had witnessed a miracle, and they were thrilled to overflowing. They had an eager anticipation that Jesus would soon be crowned King.

Around 8:00 p.m., Jesus told them to take the boat and cross over the lake. Jesus felt the need to spend time alone with His Father in heaven.

This account is found in Matthew 14:15-33. Verse 24 tells us that in the midst of the lake, suddenly contrary winds kept them from reaching their destination.

The disciples were horrified! Their rowing seemed futile. The waves were crashing against the boat. Water poured in. A catastrophe seemed imminent. If only Jesus would be there! He could help them.

Imagine working for six hours, struggling to keep the boat from capsizing. Laboring vigorously and getting nowhere.

Verse 25 tells us that in the fourth watch, around 3:00 a.m., "Jesus went unto them walking on the sea."

How quickly they forgot the miracle they previously witnessed! Now all they could see were the contrary winds, the huge waves, and now, a spirit! They cried out in desperation and fear.

Christians, too, experience contrary winds. Frequently after a person experiences a great victory, or a great blessing, suddenly one is faced with very different circumstances.

Contrary winds come when least expected, sometimes very suddenly and without warning.

Conflict may be experienced when standing for truth, and can be a contrary wind.

God's purpose in allowing contrary winds is always for our eternal good; never to work against us.

Momentarily the disciples were appalled, but Jesus' words brought comfort to them. "Be of good cheer; it is I; be not afraid" (verse 27).

Just as Jesus encouraged the disciples then, He will do the same for us today. We can always be assured that contrary winds are allowed to enrich our spiritual life. We, too, can hear Jesus' words, "Be of good cheer; it is I; be not afraid."

Our reasoning may suggest that the disciples had more than their share of trouble. Only God knows, and we can count on Him to supply grace sufficient for any situation or trial.

We may be startled at the frequency of contrary winds, especially when we are doing God's will to the best of our ability. The disciples were in the center of God's will and they were following Jesus' orders. The contrary winds found them in the line of duty. They were rowing with all their might!

When the storm is real and the winds are strong in the Christian's life, we must choose how we will respond. Either we will shrink from fear or we tune our hearts to hear the comforting words of Jesus, "It is I; be not afraid."

When we experience contrary winds, Jesus does not always calm the storm. Instead, He gives peace in the midst of adversity. No power can ever conquer the power of Jesus!

Peter was among the group and he was the first to speak. He challenged Jesus. If it's You, "bid me come unto thee on the water" (verse 28). Jesus called him, and as long as Peter kept his eyes on Jesus, he walked on the water. But when he glanced at his surroundings, he began to sink. So, too, the Christian is able to live above the circumstances of life, only as he keeps his eyes on Jesus. Like Peter, we begin to sink when our attention is diverted to the waves of our circumstances.

Someone has said, "It is not what happens to us that matters, as much as what happens in us." We can choose to wallow in self-pity, but what will it profit? We can allow discouragement to take its toll and finally die spiritually. When a person accepts the unpleasant cheerfully, and keeps from complaining, he lives in God's favor. "Do all things without murmurings and disputings" (Philippians 2"14). We do ourselves a favor and experience the blessing of being an example for others to follow and a testimony of victory to those around us, when we accept and adjust to the contrary winds howling around us.

Contrary winds may come in the form of physical sickness, the loss of a loved one, disappointment, being misunderstood or mistreated, or financial setbacks. God can use these contrary winds to help us evaluate our course in life before we meet sudden destruction.

God uses adverse circumstances to increase our faith. He allows misfortune to prepare us for His work and to make our lives more fruitful. Even though the storms may momentarily obscure our view of Christ, God still sees what is happening.

Because of the storm, the disciples experienced Jesus' power and peace. God allows our circumstances for our own joy and fulfillment. Not that we joy in the circumstances, but in God's perfect will. Through this He gives us a proper perspective. He wants us to learn to rest in His will, even though we do not understand.

God desires to reveal His power to us. It is through adversity that we grow stronger spiritually. God knows how much we can endure. He also uses our lives during adverse times to touch the lives of other people. Sometimes our tears water other people's spiritual gardens. How we face the storms that threaten our destruction is important.

At times God allows other people to make wrong choices that bring hurt to us, in order to work in our lives for our eternal good. Keeping our eyes on Jesus is the key to victorious living in every situation of life. It is also the remedy for self-exaltation and pride.

The disciples persevered. They toiled six long hours that night. The storm was severe. The storms we face may also seem severe, but we, too, must persevere. Job said, "But he knoweth the way that I take: when he hath tried me; I shall come forth as gold" (Job 23:10). Job is a good example of perseverance.

God uses contrary winds to conform us to the image of His dear Son, Jesus. Affliction and physical suffering is often His method. In all that happens to His children, God's purpose is to bring glory to Himself, encourage and strengthen other believers, and cause unbelievers to believe in Him. Nothing gets the attention of an unbeliever like a saint who suffers patiently and comes through victorious.

God asks us to take only one day at a time, one circumstance, whether joyful or adverse. By dragging yesterday's problems and borrowing from tomorrow, we become weighed down and unable to see God in each situation. The Lord intended His grace to be sufficient for this day, and with tomorrow's unknown, we have the assurance that He will again provide sufficient grace.

God's purpose is that contrary winds work for our eternal good.

What is Victory?

We cannot share victory
  unless we are victorious (Romans 8:39).
We are not victorious
  until we love the Lord with all our being (Matthew 22:37).
We cannot love God wholeheartedly
  until we know Him as Master of our life (Philippians 3:10).
We do not know Him
  until His will becomes our delight (Psalm 40:8).
His will is not our will
  until we are risen in newness of life (Colossians 3:1).
We cannot rise with Him
  until we have been crucified with Him (Galatians 2:20).
"Nevertheless I live, yet not I, but Christ"
          That is Victory!

14
Lasting Commitment

Daniel and his three friends, Shadrach, Meshach, and Abednego, were men of commitment. They would not be moved from loyalty and obedience to God, even when their lives were at stake. The record of their steadfastness is found in the Book of Daniel, chapters 1-3.

These four young men were taken captive by King Nebuchadnezzar to Babylon, where they were put in training for the king's service. He provided them, along with others of the captives, food from the king's table. But this food conflicted with God's dietary laws. And so their commitment was tested.

They asked permission to enjoy their healthy diet of fruits and vegetables, rather than the king's diet of wine and meat. God honored their commitment and blessed them with healthier bodies than those of their peers. In addition, God granted them knowledge and skill in whatever the king required of them. Daniel was given an extra portion of wisdom because of his commitment to God.

During the course of time, King Nebuchadnezzar built a huge golden idol ninety feet tall and nine feet in diameter in the Plain of Dura. He then commanded all people to bow and worship this idol.

Shadrach, Meshach, and Abednego knew from experience that to live by commitment to God was the only way to live. When the command to bow was given, they did not bow. In their hearts, they knew the true God was the only God to whom they should bow down and worship. They would not go back on their commitment to God.

The king had respect for these three young men, and he respected their God, but this time his command had to be obeyed. Everyone was to bow to the idol or be thrown into a fiery furnace.

Since they were committed to God, these young men told the king, "Be it known unto thee, O king, that we will not serve thy gods, nor worship the golden image which thou hast set up."

The king became exceedingly angry—so angry, in fact, that his attitude changed to antagonism. He commanded the furnace to be heated seven times hotter than usual, and to have these three whom he had earlier respected thrown into the fire. The fire was so hot that it killed those men who threw them into the furnace. But it did not consume them. Not long after they were thrown in, the king saw four men, loose and walking around in the fire, and "the form of the fourth [was] like the Son of God" (Daniel 3:25).

God blessed them in their commitment. They did not know whether God would spare their lives, but they were determined to serve only God, even though it may cost their lives. Their commitment was a life or death matter—they were willing to die, but God gave them life.

Commitment means "a pledge; a binding promise or agreement" (Webster). Even though in our society commitments are no longer taken so seriously, that does not change God's Word. God's Word is forever settled in heaven (Psalm 119:89). To the Christian, a commitment is still a pledge, a binding promise or agreement. It was so in the

Old Testament, and it is so today.

Satan tested Jesus' commitment to His Father through three temptations (Matthew 4:1-11). He came to Him after forty days of fasting when Jesus was physically weak. Satan offered Jesus the kingdoms of the world, if He would only bow down and worship him. Perhaps Jesus could come into His kingly power without enduring the cross. But Jesus refused. To each temptation, He answered, "It is written." In doing this, He became our perfect example of one who held true to His commitment.

Satan still comes to the Christian and tempts him to break his commitment to Christ. "Does God really mean what He says?" With every temptation, the answer can be, "It is written." God's Word has the answer to every question one faces. And like Jesus, the Christian's response must be simple, but firm. "Get thee hence, Satan: for it is written." (Matthew 4:10).

To genuinely tell Satan to depart, as did Jesus, is a sign of spiritual maturity. It is an indication of the full appropriation of Christ's authority in the life of the believer.

In Ephesians 6:10 and 11, God tells us how to withstand Satan. "Be strong in the Lord, and in the power of his might. Put on the whole armor of God, that ye may be able to stand against the wiles of the devil."

In many areas we may be tempted to weaken or fail in our commitment to our Lord, but the whole armor of God is a sure defense against the enemy.

Our speech is one such area. When with a friend, we may be tempted to speak critically or to slander another person. Our commitment calls on us to build up and to encourage, not to tear down and to damage another's reputation.

One may be tempted to give up purity of body for a few moments of so-called pleasure. But our bodies are the temple of the Holy Spirit and must be properly clothed and kept holy for God, whose we are (I Corinthians 6:19, 20).

Available reading materials may test our commitment, even when we are not aware we are being tested. The newspaper may seem more interesting, or the novel more exciting, than the reading of God's Word. If that is our experience, we will be drawn away from our commitment to God. We need to commit ourselves to a daily reading of God's Word, meditation, and prayer. Remember, it is the person who is saturated with God's Word that will have a calm, wholesome outlook on life, and whose commitment to God will be deep and lasting.

Becoming overly involved in business, or even in keeping an immaculate house, can draw us away from our primary commitment. The commitment of first teaching and training our children is what God will hold us responsible for. After all, children are the only treasures we have that have eternal value.

Misplaced loyalties undermine our commitment. We may be tempted to move away from what was once held to be right for fear of feeling out of step. We must always remember that our first loyalty is to God and His precious Word. We dare never be intimidated to move away from divine principles.

How vain we human creatures are! We want recognition. We want to be listed among "Who's Who." Often we desire our accomplishments to receive men's acclaim. Sometimes people break their commitments for no greater reward than to receive the plaudits of men.

The fear of confrontation sometimes tests our commitment. We must never become weary in well-doing. Truth must be a cherished possession. The Bible tells us to endure hardness as a good soldier of Jesus Christ.

Negative peer pressure brings pressure to bear on our commitment. People often succumb to the pressure of being outside the main stream. Peer intimidation has ruined many people. Let's be satisfied to be acceptable to God rather than to men, like the three Hebrew children and our perfect example, Jesus. To be in God's will is the safest place to be, seeking to give Him our all, and being content with the measure of success He desires for us.

Commitment is a heart issue. The first requirement in the life of a Christian is to "love the Lord thy God with all thy heart, and with all thy soul, and with all thy mind" (Matthew 22:37). This describes the commitment of Daniel and his three friends. "Keep thy heart with all diligence; for out of it are the issues of life" (Proverbs 4:23).

God has promised to keep the committed one "in perfect peace, whose mind is stayed on Him; because he trusts in Him" (Isaiah 26:3). It is in the mind that we have our thoughts, and that is where Satan entices us with wrong or unholy imaginations. Questionable thoughts produce evil thinking; evil thinking produces evil speech; and these produce bad habits and a weak, unstable character.

In contrast, the heart that is governed by God's Spirit and is pure will be faithful in all circumstances. Then the thoughts will be focused on God, the speech will be encouraging to all who hear, and these produce holy and godly character.

Commitment leads to a life of pure, peaceful, and joyful living. Its failure begins with questionable thoughts, and it results in a selfish life. In the end that life yields to Satan's allurements, and ultimately to ungodliness.

Commitment means doing what we have promised to do regardless of the consequences, even long after the mood for doing it may be gone.

The Beatitudes
Matthew 5:3-12, Paraphrased

Blessed is the woman who recognizes her deep spiritual poverty, and feels her great need. She continually draws from God's endless resources.

Blessed is the woman who realizes she must keep her eyes on Jesus. Though she mourns for her past sins and is touched by the sins of others, she rejoices in the comfort of the Holy Spirit. Through tears she experiences new horizons opening to her.

Blessed is the woman who has a holy concept of God. She realizes her sufficiency is in God, not in herself. She rejoices that God can use her and has promised to meet all of her needs.

Blessed is the woman who hungers and thirsts after God. Not only does she read His word, but earnestly and eagerly applies His word to her life. God is her life.

Blessed is the woman who is merciful and full of compassion. She is deeply touched by hurts and sorrows around her. She remembers with gratitude the merciful kindness extended to her by God and others.

Blessed is the woman who has a pure and clean heart, for she knows God dwells there. Regardless of the circumstances, she can see God in every detail of life.

Blessed is the woman who is a maker and maintainer of peace, for she knows that as she is a peacemaker will she be called one of God's children.

Blessed is the woman who can live cheerfully through misunderstandings, even if it means being persecuted for righteousness sake. She knows that faithfulness here on earth means a home in heaven.

She can even rejoice and be at peace when people speak falsely about her and say all kinds of evil things, for it is really spoken against God.

She can be joyful, and she is supremely rich, because great is her reward in heaven.

Truly fortunate, highly privileged, fully satisfied is the woman from God's perspective.

15
Power or Peril
of Our Thinking

We might not be what we think, but what we think we surely are. "For as he thinketh in his heart, so is he" (Proverbs 23:7). Our thinking is linked with our character and experience. What we are today and what we become depends largely on the thoughts we entertain. A person is the product of his own thoughts. Thoughts form the thermostat which regulates what we accomplish in life.

If I feed my selfish and carnal desires, fleshly seeds of lust, envy, bitterness, covetousness, anger, and pride are sown. Doubt, worry, and discouragement are attitudes that shape my outlook on life.

My thought pattern is under the authority of one of two masters, either God or Satan. Satan is at enmity with God; therefore, he is out to destroy the Christian's thought life. Since Satan is there to undermine, he is the author of negative or carnal thoughts. Can't, won't, and shouldn't are attitudes that come out in words that the negative force produces. In contrast, the Spirit of God produces thoughts that encourage, edify, and build. When God controls the mind, the person has kind and helpful thoughts.

Thoughts, positive or negative, grow stronger when fertilized with constant repetition. That explains why some people are gloomy and disheartened, while others are cheerful and enthusiastic in the midst of the same difficult circumstances.

It is imperative that God's Spirit controls and regulates my thought patterns, because my body responds and reacts to the input of my mind. If I feed on doubt, anxiety, and worry, I will experience frustration throughout the day. On the other hand, when my thoughts are filled with vision, hope, and victory, I can count on the blessing of being able to meet any obstacle victoriously by God's grace. What I feed grows! The mind must be renewed in order to experience power and victory.

"I beseech you therefore, brethren, by the mercies of God, that ye present your bodies a living sacrifice, holy, acceptable unto God, which is your reasonable service. And be not conformed to this world: but be ye transformed by the renewing of your mind, that ye may prove what is that good, and acceptable, and perfect, will of God" (Romans 12:1, 2). The love of God that initiated Jesus' redeeming work makes it possible for us "to become the sons of God" (John 1:12).

The mind is referred to as the workshop of the soul. It is there that aspirations, inspirations, and convictions are formed. God's love and His power produce sound, sane, and sensible thoughts in our minds. II Timothy 1:7 says, "For God did not give us a spirit of timidity—of cowardice, of craven, and cringing, and fawning fear—but...of power and of love and a calm, well-balanced mind, discipline, and self-control" (The Amplified Bible). Allowing envy, jealousy, hatred, or pride to invade our thoughts is a sure way to a mental breakdown.

Consider for a moment the root of any sinful habit. The

root always lies in the thought life, or in the mind. Entertain evil thoughts and sins such as anger, pride, lust, envy, or even unhealthy fantasizing will become part of real life. It is important that we practice consistent Bible meditation and memorization so that our minds are occupied with wholesome thinking.

Throughout Scripture we are exhorted to "gird up" our minds (I Peter 1:13)—to "brace up [your] minds, be sober" (Amplified); "to renew our minds" (Romans 12:2); and "to think on things that are true, honest, just, and pure" (Philippians 4:8). We are promised victory over sinful thoughts as we meditate on God's Word day and night (Psalm 1:2b).

When we are willing and obedient, we will make effort to focus our attention on the basic yet simple truths of the Bible. Then by God's grace and power, we can conquer sinful thoughts as we meet God's conditions for a pure and holy life. Since the mind is the foundation of the character, if we harbor the slightest thoughts of sin, we are unable to have great and lofty thoughts of God.

Our mind can be compared to a garden. We must be diligent in keeping the garden free from weeds. Galatians 6:7 reminds us: "Be not deceived; God is not mocked: for whatsoever a man soweth, that shall he also reap." We cannot expect to think thoughts of lust, envy, and covetousness and then reap a bountiful harvest of joy, love, and peace. The fruit of our lives grows in the soil of our thought lives. When our minds are renewed (Romans 12:2), God blesses us with both pure seeds and good soil. The fruit will be love, joy, peace, longsuffering, gentleness, meekness, and self-control (Galatians 5:22).

If, on the other hand, we allow our attention to become diverted and let our guard down, fleshly seeds of lust, envy, bitterness, covetousness, sensuality, anger, pride, and an unforgiving spirit are sown. These can blight our experience, causing our lives to be miserable and unproductive, and disappointing to God.

Living in defeat does not need to be our experience. If we focus our attention on God and His holiness, we can live victoriously and by God's grace can conquer the sins of the mind. Then our lives can be fruitful and productive.

Since our thought patterns affect different areas of our lives, it is imperative that our minds are disciplined in order to experience continual victory. When we experience defeat in our thoughts, we will also experience defeat in our spiritual lives. Carefulness must be exercised in our thoughts, because our thoughts can change into words that burst out at untimely and unguarded moments. Our attitudes and words are formed by the thoughts we think.

A man is what he thinks about all day long. Therefore, when God controls the thoughts, a peaceful freedom is experienced, and God can be glorified in our lives.

"Thou wilt keep him in perfect peace, whose mind is stayed on thee: because he trusteth in thee" (Isaiah 26:3).

> *Sow a thought and reap an action;*
> *Sow an action and reap a habit;*
> *Sow a habit and reap a character;*
> *Sow a character and reap a destiny.*

As a wife–
stay in your husband's
shadow. That way you
are never too far away
to encourage.

Jeremiah 9:24-25
(paraphrased)

Let not the beautiful woman glory in her pretty face or figure, neither the immaculate housekeeper glory in her ability: let not the woman of hospitality glory in her good cooking or homey atmosphere, nor the writer glory in her accomplishments.

But rather let her that glorieth glory in this, that she knows God and is growing in His wisdom and understanding of His will.

16
Eve, the First Lady

Ellen was President Wilson's first lady. They resided in Staunton, Virginia, about twelve miles from our hometown. Ellen was the most influential person in her husband's life. She encouraged him in his talents and abilities and commended his ideals. Even though she had many artistic interests, she devoted much of her time to making a comfortable home so her husband could relax from his strenuous workload.

President George Washington's home was also located in Virginia. Martha, George's first lady, managed the President's home with dignity and grace. She did not enjoy the publicity of being first lady. Many people called her Lady Washington. Martha dressed so plainly and simply that often people imagined her to be a family maid. She was a true counterpart to the President and shared his hardships. Martha organized a women's sewing circle and often mended clothes for the needy (excerpts from Virginia history).

The once famous are quickly forgotten to fade into the mist of oblivion. But Eve, the first lady, will be remembered as long as the world stands. She was the first lady created and formed by God's own fingers. She was literally built by God Himself.

The story of the first lady is found in Genesis 1-3. Genesis means beginning. It was the beginning of the creation, these beautiful surroundings which we so often take for granted. Everything was created by the spoken word of God.

When God created Adam, the first human being, the Bible tells us "God formed man of the dust of the ground and breathed into his nostrils the breath of life; and man became a living soul" (Genesis 2:7).

God then proceeded to plant a garden, preparing a home for this man that He had created. It was the most beautiful garden imaginable. God created, "every tree that was pleasant for the sight and good for food." He provided for all of Adam's needs, including the first lady.

The Bible tells us that while Adam slept God took a rib from Adam's side and formed a woman. God did not take part of Adam's foot, so he would trample over her; neither did God take a portion of Adam's brain so she would rule over him. Rather, God took a rib, close to Adam's heart, and created a woman, a true counterpart, one that would complement Adam. Eve was to be a blessing to Adam, one who would be influential like Ellen Wilson or Martha Washington who willingly shared their lives with their respective husbands.

Unlike any other woman, Eve was created perfect, sinless, pure, and holy. There was no flaw in Eve's character. Neither was there any human weakness in Adam. They were the perfect couple.

They lived in a perfect paradise, a place of bliss, felicity, and delight. It was a most beautiful Eden with no cloudy days, no rain, thunder, or lightning. Instead God created a mist that kept the garden lush and green (Genesis 2:6).

The most significant thing about their life was that they

were privileged to meet with God and commune with Him personally every evening.

But guess what! Eve was not satisfied with their blessings and the restrictions God placed before them.

Eve must have been wandering aimlessly around the garden. She must have had a hint of discontent in her life, because the Bible tells us Satan, through the form of a serpent, talked to her. "Yea, hath God said?" "Does God really mean what He says?"

In this perfect setting, God placed some restrictions for Adam and Eve. "God commanded the man saying, "Of every tree . . . thou mayest freely eat: but of the tree of the knowledge of good and evil, thou shalt not eat of it: for in the day thou eatest thereof, thou shalt surely die" (Genesis 2:16, 17).

God created this perfect couple with the power of choice, and they chose to disobey Him. Adam and Eve deliberately disregarded God's instructions and willfully chose to listen to His and their enemy.

Eve, that perfect specimen of womanhood, was not content with her perfect lot. Satan knew her tint of dissatisfaction. Ever since, Satan still uses the same strategy. He tempts us where we are the weakest and the most vulnerable.

Through disobedience (tasting of the forbidden fruit) they experienced spiritual death. The first thing they did was try to cover their bodies with fig leaves. Then they tried to hide from God. Because of their disobedience, they became afraid of God, the One who had created them and with whom, just hours before, they had had such sweet communion.

It must have brought a deep sadness to God's heart. Now He had to remove them from this secure and serene setting.

Adam needed to work hard for food for himself, his wife, and future family. Eve was to be submissive to her husband. She would suffer pain and in sorrow she would become a mother. Tears and heartache would now be part of their experience.

Adam named his wife Eve because she was "the mother of all living" (Genesis 3:20).

A Bible storybook depicts Adam and Eve leaving this lovely Garden of Eden. Both are crying. Adam's arm is around Eve and they are walking out into a dark unknown. Behind them are angels with flaming swords that turn every way to keep them from returning to this beautiful garden of bliss and serenity.

I am deeply grateful the story does not end with a sad and hopeless note. Instead, God, the holy, merciful, and just Creator of the universe, had a plan to redeem His creation back to Himself. Genesis 4:1, tells us that when Eve's first baby was born she said, "I have gotten a man from the Lord" Already she was looking forward to the Savior who would restore womanhood and bring peace between God the Creator and Eve His creation.

Eve, the first lady, was designed by God and was created for His glory. She was truly a woman from God's perspective, until she chose to disobey.

Instead of enjoying God's many blessings, we all too often focus on the forbidden or that which God has not given us. Guidelines and rules have always been part of God's plan. They never deprive people of joyful and fulfilled lives, but rather make them possible. God places principles and commandments throughout the Bible to guide people to deeper commitment and greater joy and fulfillment.

Womanhood is never all it should be, unless God has His rightful place in our lives. Jesus' sacrifice on Calvary makes it possible for us to once again be restored to God the Creator, and to have peace and contentment in our hearts.

I wonder where Adam was when Eve began to focus on the forbidden tree? Why did he permit the serpent to talk to his wife? Why was Eve discontented and focused on the forbidden tree rather than being thankful? They had all their hearts could desire.

Years later Eve's nature of discontent is very prevalent in my own heart. Human nature is to wish for the forbidden, to make myself believe I'd be happy if —. Contentment is a life-long pursuit. We must allow Jesus to have first place in our hearts. That is the key to contentment.

Instead of a thankful spirit prevailing, we tend to focus on what we don't have. We spend time looking at our neighbors, sometimes wishing we had what they have. We see them sitting on their porch enjoying the night sounds. Either we become discontent with our workload or we are glad for them that they can enjoy this leisure.

Another neighbor is getting a new living room suite. Are we happy for them, or are we envious?

Other neighbors are working in the garden, enjoying a pleasant evening together. We can rejoice with them that they enjoy working together as a family, or we may lament all the weeds in our garden, or that our children are grown and gone.

Often we must choose whether we will live within God's will for our lives or focus on the prohibited (that which is not God's will for our lives). Many times we must choose whether we will rejoice or crave experiences that God gives another. It all depends on our heart attitude.

"Blessed are the pure in heart for they shall see God [in everything]" (Matthew 5:8).

Three surgeries in eighteen months and twenty weeks of recuperation have been my lot. God has been breaking my will by placing His perfect will before me. He wants me to view God's many blessings from the recliner, while other women are busy working, traveling, shopping, or just simply enjoying good health. I must choose how I will accept the limitations, pain, and recovery. I choose whether I will praise the Lord for the little unnoticed blessings, or whether I will yearn for the forbidden and complain.

In my pastor husband's life, besides working for a living, he is called on to counsel and encourage fellow church members. When his workload becomes heavy and tiring, I choose whether I'll add to that pressure or whether I will pray and encourage him in obedience to God.

The story of Eve is a good lesson for us in the twentieth century. Because she focused on the forbidden, she lost her perfect state with her Maker. We need not make the same mistake. God's Word gives us guidelines and rules to follow which instead of making us discontent and envious bring us into perfect peace with God. "The fear of God tendeth to life: and he that hath it shall abide satisfied" (Proverbs 19:23). The fear of God is generally missing in society. But we are promised God will fully satisfy us as we seek His way and love Him with a pure heart. A thankful, contented spirit governs the restored life.

God knows the human heart and one's whole being. He also knows that the amazing capacity for God can never be satisfied with a substitute. The heart is only fulfilled as the God-shaped vacuum is filled by God Himself.

Psalm 16:11 is the testimony of a fulfilled woman, one who has given God His rightful place. "In thy presence is fulness of joy; at thy right hand there are pleasures forever-more." Living in God's presence is the safest place to be. It is integral in a restored life of womanhood.

It is in the shadow of the cross of Jesus that exchanges take place.

Discontentment< >Contentment – "I have learned, in whatsoever state I am, therewith to be content" (Philippians 4:11).

Envy< >the joy of the Lord – "The joy of the LORD is your strength" (Nehemiah 8:10b).

My weakness< >God's strength – "For when I am weak, then I am strong" (II Corinthians 12:10).

Frustration< >God's peace – "Thou wilt keep [her] in perfect peace . . . because [she] trusteth in thee" (Isaiah 26:3).

Covetousness< >Thankfulness – "In every thing give thanks: for this is the will of God" (I Thessalonians 5:18).

Deceit and Hypocrisy< >Meekness and Gentleness – "Blessed are the meek" (Matthew 5:5).

My will< >God's will – "Nevertheless not as I will, but as thou wilt" (Matthew 26:39).

Self-exaltation< >Servant's heart – "Whosoever will be chief among you, let him be your servant" (Matthew 20:27).

Self-sufficiency and self-confidence< >Christ's suffi-ciency and capability – "I can do all things through Christ, which strengtheneth me" (Philippians 4:13).

As these exchanges become our experience, we become women from God's perspective and are again restored to wholeness that pleases God.

Maturity is when –

You finish a job without supervision.
You can have money in your pocket without spending it.
You can receive a slight or injustice without feeling the need to retaliate.
You hold firmly to God's Truth.
You share liberally what God has shared with you.
You can pray fervently for those who oppose you.
You can do good to those who treat you unfairly or maliciously.
These are the marks of Christian maturity!

17

The Hidden Wife
in Noah's Life

There are only five verses in the Bible that refer to Noah's wife. She is mentioned only as being present with Noah and their sons with their wives. There is no record of her except that she was the wife of the hero of the flood. She went with him into the ark. The account is found in Genesis 6-9.

Like her husband, who was a just man and had God's approval on his life, she, too, must have had a deep and reverent consciousness of God. In fact, it is very possible that she was with Noah when God spoke to him and gave the assignment.

Her character is reflected in her family line, which continued strong for over three hundred years after the flood (Genesis 9:28).

It is also interesting to note that the Bible does not indicate that Noah's wife had part in his experience of making wine and becoming drunk. If she had been living, she may have saved him from this embarrassment that blotted his life.

Noah is repeatedly praised in Scripture as a devoted man of God. But standing in his shadow was a pious, nameless woman about whom nothing is ever said. She is simply known as Noah's wife.

Consider for a moment the extraordinary qualities this hidden woman must have possessed. She must have experienced a deep and lasting relationship with God. One Bible storybook depicts Noah and his wife kneeling with folded hands looking into heaven while God's rays of approval shone around them as a couple.

She must have been an extremely patient person. How else could she have endured the mocking and ridicule of her family and friends? Many times she must have cringed while hearing whisperings at the marketplace. She must have had an exceptionally understanding, loving, and supportive heart in order to encourage Noah in his most unusual task.

God blessed them with three sons, Shem, Ham, and Japheth.

Noah was called of God to construct this unheard of boat even though it had never rained before. This added to the uniqueness of this test of faith. God also called Noah to preach and warn the people of impending judgment. In II Peter 2:5, Noah was called a preacher of righteousness. Beside all this, he also needed to provide for his family.

For one hundred and twenty years, this hidden woman stood with her husband as he answered God's call to build the ark and to preach. And during this same century, Noah's wife was a loyal, faithful mother to her three sons.

During this assignment, she was a wise, sensible, and prudent woman. She kept her eyes on the goal, God's purpose for her family. She also must have had a real desire to see others saved from the flood.

Because of her noble character, she could instill the same godly traits in the boys' lives. Her godly influence brought stability to the boys so they were also able to withstand the strain and inevitable pressures they faced from their peers.

Because of Noah's and his wife's undivided loyalty to God and each other, they were able to find suitable wives for their sons. These three young women saw more than did the rest of the population. Their contact with Noah's family brought them to a knowledge of the God of Noah.

While Noah was finishing the interior, building various rooms for all the animals and a suitable home for his family, Mrs. Noah was building rooms of lasting value: rooms of kindness, unselfishness, forbearance, acceptance, order, peace, contentment, gentleness, and joy. While Noah sealed the inside and outside with pitch to make the ark waterproof, Noah's wife was decorating the walls of the ark with love and security for her family.

Today, many centuries later, God is still calling on each husband to provide an ark of protection for his family. It is to be a haven from this hostile society in which God has placed us. The blood of Jesus provides that ark of protection. Where Jesus' blood is applied, there will be a haven where father, mother, and children seek God's approval and blessing. The Bible becomes the guide of life, and following God's blueprint becomes most important.

Noah and his wife were able to rear healthy, well-taught, secure children in a very wicked and busy society.

The same grace of God is available today to godly parents to rear healthy, well-taught, secure children.

Noah and his wife must have woven love, warmth, a sense of joy, fulfillment, and a mutual parental support in their busy schedules.

We can assume they encouraged good behavior, but did not eliminate punishment for bad behavior. They clearly and simply enforced God's principles in everyday living. There were rules to live by, and they guarded their children with jealous care.

They were able to save their family from the wrath of God's judgment because they lived so close to God that they knew His will for their lives. The whole family understood that their protection was within the ark.

Positive attitudes and grateful spirits, rather than negative ones, dictated their lives. Since Noah and his wife were faithful to God and each other, they could command faithful obedience from their boys.

They exercised divine love and fairness within their small cottage; therefore, it became a "hot-bed" environment that reached out with compassion for their friends and neighbors.

Since they lived lives worthy of honor, respect, and obedience, they took their parental responsibilities seriously and of foremost importance.

Someone made the statement, "Rearing children is like holding a wet bar of soap in your hand. Grasp it too tightly or too loosely and you lose it." Noah and his wife are a good example of having a proper hold on their boys. Because of their faithfulness and obedience to God, they were able to bring significance, security, and serenity— three ingredients that are still needed today for healthy relationships within the family.

Noah and his wife shared the same heartbeat; therefore they experienced God's wisdom and knowledge. Their ways were discreet and blameless because they received their directions from God; therefore their words were full of encouragement and compassion. They didn't have time to complain or criticize.

Mrs. Noah's years of commitment and personal sacrifice so that God's work could be accomplished by her husband paid off. She was blessed to see the faithfulness of her sons and their wives. Her character is reflected in her family's lives three centuries later.

Even though she was the nameless wife of Noah, she filled her place well in the transition from the old world to the new. For every woman there is a work God has for her to fulfill. The women God can use are diligent and faithful in God's kingdom, whether they are known or unknown.

The Successful Husband / Wife Team

1. *Have God as the focal point (Proverbs 3:5, 6).*
2. *Spend time together in studying God's Word and praying for each other and other needs.*
3. *Have clear-cut responsibilities. Know what is required of each teammate.*
4. *Be an encourager. Be appreciative. If you have a criticism, don't just gripe. Kindly suggest what might be done to improve the situation.*
5. *Talk about issues you disagree on in a private place. Remember God is always present. He is disappointed when we are disrespectful to each other.*
6. *Learn to laugh at yourself.*
7. *Give in to your partner. Remember you need the different perspectives that your spouse can lend. Have a teachable spirit. No one knows it all, but together God can be glorified.*

This is the harness and yoke that will enable you to pull together harmoniously.

"Trust in the Lord, and do good...Delight thyself also in the Lord; and he shall give thee the desires of thine heart" (Psalm 37:3, 4).

18

The Twentieth Century Total Woman

When I think of vigorous activity and genuine rest, I remember the story of Martha and Mary (Luke 10:38-42). Martha was frantically dashing about getting the last minute touches on a delicious meal she was preparing for the special guest, Jesus. All the while Mary was at ease, sitting at Jesus' feet, admiringly drinking in His words of life. Martha is portrayed as an over-extended server, while Mary is commended for choosing the best.

Bethany was a quiet little town about two miles from Jerusalem, on the east slope of the Mt. of Olives. (See map of Palestine.) In this little town lived Martha, Mary, and their brother Lazarus. It must have been a homey, well-kept cottage, clean, cool, and refreshing. Jesus knew He was always welcome when He passed through the area. We observe in John 12 and Luke 10 that Jesus loved to visit and relax in their home. The Bible tells us these four were closely acquainted and enjoyed time together (John 11:15).

Martha may have been a widow who owned the neat little cottage, while Lazarus and Mary both felt secure in this arrangement.

Martha, a diligent housekeeper, was busy serving.

Apparently preparing a delicious meal was her goal. She probably knew Jesus' favorite dishes, and to Him she was giving her best.

Mary, in contrast, showed her love and devotion by sitting at Jesus' feet and learning from Him.

In Martha's life, tangible commitment took first place rather than the intangible attitudes of worship.

Martha felt baffled that Mary did not share her goal, so she complained to Jesus. "Jesus, don't You see I'm serving by myself. Tell Mary to help me complete the preparations."

The answer that Jesus gave still rings clear today. "Mary hath chosen that good part which shall not be taken away from her." Jesus' rebuke to Martha was not undermining the importance of work; rather, He is teaching the importance of being the total woman from God's perspective. (John 12:1-8 records that Mary did serve Jesus another time.)

Jesus redirected Martha's attention from activity and serving to exclusive and concentrated loyalty. Undivided loyalty to Christ, whether in quiet worship or active service, is acceptable to God. As twentieth century total women, our love and devotion includes our activity as well as all of our thinking and all of our worship. The total woman needs to be a Mary-Martha.

Since God is too great to be compared with, it is imperative to grow in His knowledge and likeness. By living in the "fear of the LORD all the day long" (Proverbs 23:17), we will be able to be His total woman. "The fear of the LORD is the beginning of knowledge" (Proverbs 1:7). "That in the ages to come he might show the exceeding riches of his grace in his kindness toward us through Christ Jesus" (Ephesians 2:7). We find ourselves living in a hurried society, but God did not make a mistake when He placed us in our environment. Rather, we have the privilege to serve Him in spite of our surroundings. God surrounds us by the exceeding riches of His grace, as we live in His fear. The description of fear is not dread but a wholesome awe of His person. It is the attribute found in a person with a pure heart. Therefore God will be clearly seen in every situation.

We sometimes find ourselves asking the question, Is there serenity within this hassled world? I Corinthians 14:33 reminds us that "God is not the author of confusion, but of peace." He is a God of order, and where there is order, there is peace.

The creation account found in Genesis 1, 2 records an orderly process. The twentieth century woman should be a Mary-Martha, a woman of order, an industrious and a worshipful woman.

Since God is a God of order, He also is a God of time and eternity. Everyone has been allotted the same amount of time—twenty-four hours in each day, sixty minutes in each hour. We will not feel cheated or frustrated because God in His wisdom has wisely designed life for us with our good in mind.

"For God has not given us the spirit of fear [or cowardliness], but of power [to do his will], and of love [charity like that in John 3:16], and of a sound mind [a well-balanced, calm mind that is disciplined and self-controlled]." It is within this realm that the total woman can face life and handle the many duties God would have her perform.

It is within the bounds of God's enabling power to make the best use of our time. We must evaluate what is most important and not allow the seemingly urgent to cloud our thinking.

Daily we need to pray that God would teach us to number our days (Psalm 90:12), so we are able to make use of the opportunities that come our way only once. There may be times we must say, "No" in order to do well what God has assigned.

God's enabling power is available when our already busy schedule requires visiting the sick or the discouraged. We need to learn the art of doing small jobs in spare minutes. What about those few moments we wait for a phone call to go through? What about the minutes we wait for our husbands, when the meals are ready and waiting? There are minutes here and there that, if used wisely, will lessen the tension and pressure later!

What about those quiet Sunday afternoons that could be used in writing a letter or note of encouragement? Giving fifteen minutes of one's time could make a world of difference in someone's day.

The power of God enables us to learn to plan on the run. Learn to appreciate minute rests and vacations. Take time to observe the growth of the flowers or watch the development of a rosebud. Tune your ears to hear the musical songs of the frogs or birds.

Keep things picked up, pulled out, and put in their proper place. On your way to the mailbox, while looking up, also observe items that may litter the landscape. What better exercise than to stop and pick them up.

Short and long term goals help us to use our time wisely, but we must always remember to do the will of God.

When God's enabling power is working, our lives will be full of agape love. This love affects the way we use our time and talents. When love is at the root, it will flavor everything we do because "the love of Christ constraineth us" (II Corinthians 5:14).

A sound mind includes pure, holy, and clean thinking.

Unless our heart is pure, our mind will not be disciplined and self-controlled. It is the mind that prompts worship, the kind of worship found in Isaiah 26:3: "Thou wilt keep [her] in perfect peace, whose mind is stayed on thee: because [she] trusteth in thee."

The Mary heart of worship and the Martha heart of service is where true fulfillment is found.

Hospitality was present in the neat and homey little cottage in Bethany years ago. Hospitality still marks the total woman's home in the twentieth century. Since it is the heart that welcomes, the house does not have to be of latest style or fashionable interior decorating. A loving, orderly, clean environment is adequate. Hospitality is a gift not all women possess. It is a virtue that all must strive to exercise, although for some it may be easier than for others. It is making a home away from home for visitors. It is where people like to be, because they feel refreshed.

Paul, in I Corinthians 16:15-18, draws attention to the house of Stephanas. They dedicated themselves to serving the saints, and Paul mentions they refreshed him and others. This is a description of true hospitality. It is refreshing and encouraging.

If you planned soup for supper and you unexpectedly entertain guests, serve soup, but be sure it's served from a heart of love and devotion to God. Hospitality is not putting on the best, it is being our best for God's glory, because Jesus is the unseen guest at every meal, the silent listener to every conversation. Doing as unto Jesus is the key to hospitality.

Some women are tempted to feel if only they would have a larger, more convenient house, if only their children were older, if only their husbands would provide better, or if only there would be more time, then they could be hospitable. If the attitude prevails that the whole life is exclusively loyal to Christ, then the size of the house, the kind of food, the age of the children, are not the deciding factors whether we are hospitable or not.

Whatever our lot in life, we can be a Mary-Martha, and share our orderly, cozy home with others. Everyone appreciates an atmosphere where God's resources are at work— power, love, and self-control.

"That in the ages to come he might shew the exceeding riches of his grace, in his kindness toward us through Christ Jesus" (Ephesians 2:7).

Obedience
frees us to
become all God
meant for us to
become.

His Will Is Best

As I stood in the morn, at the foot of the hill,
With my spirit forlorn, but resigned to His will –
"Oh, dear Lord," I did cry, "I'm so weary today,
And the hill is so high—Is there no other way?"
Then my Shepherd replied, "Though the pathway be steep,
I'll be close by your side, and your feet I will keep.
I'll be holding your hand, and your strength I'll supply
Till at even you stand on the hilltop so high."

So together we went, with His hand upon mine
And I found sweet content in His presence divine.
Then my pathway seemed bright, as we traveled along,
For my spirit grew light, and my heart filled with song.
At the close of the day, on the summit I stood,
Looking down at the way, where my Shepherd so good
Had been leading me on; and it seemed not so steep
As it had at the dawn, nor the valley deep;
For He leveled the road, step by step, as He led,
And where dangers abode, He was always ahead.

So I learned on the hill, as I stood at the crest,
That to walk in His will is the way that is best.

-Author Unknown

19

Chastening Makes the Heart Clean

If a person is singled out to be a special object of God's grace, he may expect God to honor him with stricter discipline and greater suffering.

God is like a sculptor. He is the One who has created us and who is transforming us into the image of His dear Son. Without the painful blows and the sanding off of the rough edges, our lives would remain forever formless, without beauty, and useless. God always has our best in mind as He tests and tries us. "Now no [correction or discipline] for the present seemeth to be joyous, but grievous; nevertheless afterward it yieldeth the peaceable fruit of righteousness" (Hebrews 12:11). The fruit of righteousness consists of conforming to God's will in purpose, thought, and action. This results in right living and right standing with God.

Job is an example of one of God's children who went through stricter discipline and more suffering than many of the Bible characters. The story is found in Job Chapters 1-42. The Bible tells us he was a blameless and upright person. Job manifested a strict regard for what was morally right. He was ready to stand against the wiles of the devil. He was a man who was guiltless and faultless. Job and his family seemed to be a close family, and God had blessed them with a good relationship. Verse 4 would indicate that they spent time together, perhaps on their birthdays or holidays.

Job's character stands out in verse 1, but especially in verse 5. Job was concerned that during these "together" times his family would not sin against God. Job as a father had a deep concern, so deep, in fact, that he got up early and earnestly interceded for his children. The Bible tells us, "Thus did Job continually." He regularly offered sacrifices and pleaded to God for his children's spiritual well-being. Job had a real concern for his family. He took his responsibility seriously.

We would say Job had everything going for him; but read further in the first chapter of Job. Satan was among the ones that presented themselves to God. He also saw the blameless life Job was living (v. 6). Satan blamed God for building a hedge around Job. Satan was jealous as he is today. He is out to destroy the family unit, to bring chaos and hurt to the family.

God did grant Satan permission to test Job. "In all this, Job sinned not nor [blamed] God" (Job 1:22). His testimony is found in verse 21, "[Without possession] came I into the world, and [without possession] will I depart; the LORD gave and the LORD hath taken away: blessed be the name of the LORD."

Job lost his children and his material possessions. If Job would not have been a man of God, he could not have responded by magnifying and praising God. Job had proper priorities and he recognized them as gifts from God. He worshiped God for who He was, not for the gifts he enjoyed. The effects of stricter discipline and greater suffering upon a godly person cannot be better portrayed than in Job's life.

Satan still was not satisfied. Again he accused Job to God, and again God permitted Satan to touch him—this time his body. Boils broke out from the top of his head to the soles of his feet. The Bible tells us even his wife told him to curse God and die. What a challenging testimony – "In all this did not Job sin with his lips." Job even rebuked his wife. "What, shall we receive [only] good at the hand of God, and shall we not receive evil?"

At the time Job needed his wife most, she let him down. Job felt all alone. His children were dead; all his animals had been either killed or stolen; he was in agony; his suffering was intense; and boils were breaking out from the top of his head to the sole of his feet. He experienced pain— physical, emotional, and mental pain, the pain of loss, and now yet the pain of his wife's rejection. No wonder he felt forsaken, perhaps even by his Creator. Yet he held to his integrity.

As if that were not enough, Job's three trusted friends heard of his tragedy and came to visit him. After seven days of silence they talked. Instead of being encouragers, they condemned him because, in their way of thinking, surely a righteous person would not have all of these calamities. One of Job's friends reminded him: "They that plow iniquity, and sow wickedness, reap the same" (4:8). Even though this may be a true statement, it was not the case with Job. The statement was very much out of place.

Eliphaz, one of Job's friends, said: "Behold, happy is the man whom God correcteth; therefore despise not thou the chastening [strict discipline] of the Almighty" (5:17). Job is a true example of one who allowed the chastening of God to cleanse his heart. In all this, Job did not sin.

Job's three friends seemed to multiply his sufferings

rather than alleviating them. Even in all this adversity, Job continued to acknowledge God's holiness while he pleaded for an answer. Job portrayed a wonderful confidence and trust in his Maker. "Though he slay me, yet will I trust in him" (Job 13:15). He would remain true even though God would slay him. He had nothing left; yet, he realized that God was enough.

In all of Job's sufferings and in the midst of his poor comforters, he was able to say, "But [God] knoweth the way that I take: when he hath tried me, I shall come forth as gold" (Job 23:10). All through Job's severe trials he remained a man of integrity.

Stricter discipline for God's children, chastening that makes the heart clean, certainly is not something to ask for. But in Job's life, as well as in many other noble people's lives, stricter discipline and correction are all avenues through which God can bring out the best in a person.

Satan capitalizes on the suffering, correction, and discipline to destroy us. God chastens and corrects for our profit and for our eternal good. When we can come through trials victoriously, we will be drawn closer to God, will share in His holiness, and bear more fruit for His glory. God had a refining purpose in mind for Job, even though Satan tried his best to undermine God's plan. God also refines his people through suffering. It is not a catastrophe that God could not prevent; rather, He permits it for our purging. God's hand is in it all. Therefore, it is one of the "all things" (Romans 8:28) in which God works for our eternal good.

Any chastening, correction, and discipline God permits is intended to make us better, holier, richer in character, gentle, and more patient. There is a security in leaving to God the matter of evil committed against us. Satan is at enmity with God; therefore, we may better understand that the wrong is against God far more than against man. God is the final Judge in any matter. Our concern must be that we learn the lesson He intends for us to learn.

Stricter discipline for God's obedient children—no one would choose that. But because of success or position, there often has been a life of hardships, jealousy and envy from others, as well as loneliness. It is God's way of working to bring a person to the measure of his usefulness for God's purposes.

Abraham Lincoln has been admired by many. Yet few, if any, would choose the life of hardships that led to his honor as one of the greatest Presidents in history. His mother died when he was a young child. He worked hard and long to have enough food and clothing, and to educate himself. Nevertheless, later in life he credited his success in life to his step-mother. He stated, "All that I am I owe to my angel mother."

Elizabeth Elliot, a well-known writer and speaker, has experienced much suffering and hardships in her Christian life. Married to Jim Elliot, who was killed twenty-seven months after their marriage, she was called to rear an infant daughter in the jungles of Ecuador where she and Jim had been in mission work together. She carried on her work of translation along with many other duties. She experienced widowhood twice, and was single more years than married. Her testimony rings clear. Early in her Christian life she met Jesus at Calvary's cross. She laid her life down and accepted the stricter discipline God gives to His obedient children.

In the twentieth century, God is still calling His faithful children to a life of stricter discipline and greater suffering. When we meet Jesus at Calvary's cross, that is where two wills cross and someone must die. It is only when I choose

Jesus' will and take up His cross that I can have the confidence that even though it may cost suffering and strict discipline, life with Him is the only way to true joy and lasting fulfillment.

"Blessed are the pure in heart: for they shall see God" [in everything] (Matthew 5:8). Yes, the pure in heart are blessed by the chastening of the Lord. It makes their heart so clean and so blessed.

Careless parents
produce
heedless children.

The Fruit of the Spirit
in the Life of the Christian . . . Galatians 5:22

Love is the ingredient of the heart, that shares God with others.

Joy is the expression of the heart regardless of the circumstances.

Peace is the relationship in every phase of life, with God and man.

Long-suffering is the power to see things to completion.

Gentleness is the mild spread that lights the countenance.

Goodness is the present reality of caring, sharing, and doing.

Faith steadies the footsteps to higher places of aspiration.

Meekness finds all the strength in God and recognizes one's own inability.

Temperance orders life with discretion.

Purity is the willingness to keep the record stainless.

If we live by the Holy Spirit, we will also exercise these qualities. These are the way of life. We will not become boastful, neither will there be any envy or jealousy.

The Christian is not called to status, but to servanthood!

20

The Makings of
a Strong Family

There is no school that people can attend to learn technique of Christian family living. Families become strong because parents fear the Lord and love Him with all their hearts (read Matthew 22:34-40; 19:3-6; Mark 10:5-9). These parents live by Biblical truths in everyday life, conducting the everyday obligations in the strength of the Lord. Godly family living doesn't just happen; it is the result of domestic determination and commitment, both of which are rare in our day.

Psalm 128 declares the foundation of a strong, happy family. "Blessed, happy, fortunate, [to be envied] is everyone who fears, reverences, and worships the Lord; who walks in His ways and lives according to His commandments" (verse 1, Amplified).

Psalm 1:1, 2 also indicates that the leader in a strong family will meditate on God's love and commandments and will fear and reverence God. These are the truly happy and blessed people.

God's Word becomes the blueprint for parents to follow as God blesses them with children. Children receive teaching and training that guides them through their youthful years and finally conducts them into a responsible adult-hood. These people bring glory to God and are effective and capable of bringing blessing and encouragement to others.

Since God's Word is the final authority, it should be the aspiration of each family member to follow the Bible fully.

To love God, live in obedience, and to love each other as husband and wife is a commitment that was made on the wedding day. We promise to be faithful always whether we feel like it or not.

Strong marriages result in strong families. The commitment is to love. The question asked is not, "Do you love?" but "Will you love?" Without self-giving love there will be no strong marriage, and therefore no strong family.

God's plan for a strong family was not instituted for selfish gain; rather, for the praise and glory of God. God then blesses with many blessings known only to the obedient.

When God is at the center of the family, it will be evident in the order of the home—how business is pursued; how leisure time is spent; who is in control of time, talents, and possessions; and even how vacations are spent. It is also evident how disappointment is faced. If God is at the center in these areas, our gaze will be fixed on Him continually, for His divine approval.

What makes a strong family? It is the agape love that keeps the promises and commitments made to each other as husband and wife. It is time spent together in worship, work, and leisure. It is a relaxed, open, and conducive communication that is God-centered, and conversation that encourages and shares appreciation with family members to the extent that problems are solved and differences resolved as they arise. All these are attitudes that contribute to a strong family. God is the foundation of every fruitful life, and when members are all faithful, God's blessing becomes the key to strong relationships.

It is the fear of God that rules the strong family; therefore all other fears are dismissed. God's fear motivates, gives direction, and gives security. "But be thou in the fear of the LORD all the day long" (Proverbs 23:17b). "The fear of the LORD is the beginning of knowledge" (Proverbs 1:7). The fear of man bringeth a snare: but whoso putteth his trust in the LORD shall be safe" (Proverbs 29:25).

God's stamp of approval on the family assures God's blessings. "Blessed is every one that feareth the LORD: that walketh in his way. For thou shalt eat the labour of thine hands: happy shalt thou be, and it shall be well with thee" (Psalm 128:1, 2). It is truly a privilege to work together as a family and to enjoy the blessings of each other. This brings joy and fulfillment. It makes burdens lighter when shared, and multiplies the joys and happiness. Within this context the wife and mother finds contentment and satisfaction in fulfilling the menial daily tasks. The husband finds fulfillment in meeting the family's emotional, spiritual, and physical needs. The children feel secure and happy when parents complement each other.

Truly the family is blessed who reverently and worshipfully serves the Lord. Their influence reaches unto generations yet to come.

God's plan for the husband is that

- He follows God carefully and closely,
- he resists evil,
- he is gentle and loving, yet firm,

- he is understanding, respectful, and morally faithful,
- he works hard and is honest,
- he is sensitive and gives generously,
- he leads his wife and family in daily worship,
- by example he teaches his children,
- he understands and chooses God's way.

God's plan for the wife is that

- she is devoted to God and her family,
- she is a keeper at home,
- she has a meek and quiet spirit,
- she has a strong faith in God,
- she has time for her family,
- by example she trains her children,
- she submits to her husband,
- she practices modesty and is content with simplicity,
- she has an inner beauty and has natural order and neatness,
- she shares and gives to those in need.

Selfishness makes us angry,
Blame makes us bitter,
Self-pity makes us lonely,
BUT
Committed love makes us strong!

The commitment that preserves a strong family—

By God's grace, we will love God with all our heart.
By God's grace, we will love each other sacrificially.
By God's grace, we will guide our children wisely.
By God's grace, we will serve the church faithfully.

Stories may perish, song be forgot,
But a graven record, time changes not.
Whatever is written on the heart of a child
Whether heaven has blessed or earth has defiled,
A story of gladness or care,
Will linger unchangeably there.

—Author Unknown

Come Home

The Word of God teaches us as wives,
In everything to submit ourselves
To our husbands as unto the Lord,
And we'll live peaceably in accord.

But are we not equal? says the world,
We shouldn't let men over us lord;
We'll get a career and earn the bread,
And let the men stay home in our stead.

But homes are ruined and peace is lost.
Precious children pay the awful cost
Of broken homes and their mothers' sin.
Won't you please come home again!

Think not your lot such a humble one.
It's God's great calling for you, woman.
Keepers at home are his perfect will;
You'll be blessed, if His plan you fulfill.

Mrs. Ruth Weaver
used by permission, 1999

21
Childhood – Too Precious to Miss

Children grow up so quickly! Right now your child is developing in so many ways—physically, emotionally, and mentally. He needs strong parents who give him a good foundation as a vital part of his development.

It has been said that ninety percent of those who become Christians do so before age twenty-one. Therefore children need a sure foundation that will prepare them for the most important decision they will ever make. A Christ-centered family unit provides that foundation on which to build.

Beside salvation, the most important gift God gives to parents is children. Their childhood is too precious for parents to miss.

We must build on Jesus Christ, the solid foundation. "For other foundation can no man lay than that is laid, which is Jesus Christ" (I Corinthians 3:11). Jesus taught how important it is to have the right foundation (Matthew 7:25-27). He spoke of the wise man and the foolish man. The wise man built on the rock, while the foolish man built on the sand. The floods came and the winds blew, and beat upon the house, and it didn't fall because it was founded on a rock. The foolish man's house fell because it was built on the sand. A children's song illustrates this story and usual-ly leaves an impact on the young child's mind.

If the preciousness of children is a priority, we will want to discover what the foundations and building of the home consist of. Proverbs 9:1 tells us that, "Wisdom hath build-ed her house, she hath hewn out her seven pillars."

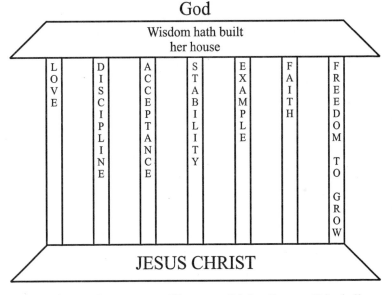

Perhaps the seven pillars could be Love, Discipline, Acceptance, Stability, Example, Faith, and the Freedom to Grow.

Love is the first pillar, but *discipline* is closely related. We know that no one can love like our heavenly Father. His love is everlasting. "I have loved thee with an everlasting love: therefore with lovingkindness have I drawn thee" (Jeremiah 31:3). Within that everlasting love there is a kindness that is just, that will not leave His children to do as they would. Proverbs 3:12 reminds us that "whom the LORD loveth he correcteth, even as a father the son in whom he delighteth." Proverbs 13:24: "He that spareth his rod hateth his son: but he that loveth him [correcteth] him [early in life]." Hebrews 12:6: "For whom the Lord loveth he [corrects and disciplines]."

When parents, from their hearts, love and cherish their children, the Bible way will become the way they take. Loving children includes loving them enough to correct them and to guide them in God's ways. Everyone enjoys obedient and responsive children. Only by a consistent love and discipline do they become that way.

Children will not grow up to be disciplined unless parents love them enough not to allow them to take their own way. Love and discipline are inseparable when teaching children to enjoy life and how to exercise self-discipline.

Setting boundaries is another expression of true love. Children who know where the limits and boundaries are have a sense of security. Having no boundaries shows a disinterest in the child, and leaves the child without proper direction.

A proper balance of love and discipline brings a healthy balance between freedom and restraint. The child is free to grow because he is able to discern right from wrong. The boundaries are placed there with his spiritual welfare in mind, and so he learns what is good and what is harmful for him.

Acceptance is the third pillar. Every individual matters to God! "I will praise thee; for I am fearfully and wonderfully made: marvelous are thy works; and that my soul knoweth right well" (Psalm 139:14). Only God can design the human body, and only God has a divine plan for each individual. Self-acceptance is possible when one has a proper concept of God, His greatness, and His holiness. Children don't just happen; they are a loving thought of

God long before conception. Self-acceptance can be taught only if children are significant to parents. They must be taught they are of God's creation and *they do matter.* Each child is uniquely precious and important.

Parents convey much to their children by their own attitudes and concept of God. Their acceptance of their children speaks louder than words.

Acceptance is also communicated by how intimately the parents are involved in the child's life. So much is transmitted when the child speaks. It takes an alert parent to truly listen and wisely hear what is being said.

Stability is the fourth pillar. Stability means the child knows that home will always be home. It is a safe place with Dad and Mom who are devoted to God and each other for the child's spiritual and physical welfare.

The story of *The Three Little Pigs* illustrates both instability and stability. Only the house that was established on a firm foundation was strong and secure. The wolf could not destroy the third pig's house. Satan can be likened to the big bad wolf. Unless our homes are stable, we will not be able to withstand the evil darts of Satan, because he is out to destroy the home. Stability begins with a solid foundation in Jesus Christ. Mom and Dad must be dedicated Christians who have their children's best interest in mind. Children need both security and stability or they will feel insecure.

Stability brings security, and both are found in the solid foundation that never changes.

Example is the fifth pillar. In I Corinthians 11:1, Paul gives a good definition of example. "Be ye followers of me, even as I also am of Christ." *Example* is defined as "one who illustrates a rule or provides practice in its application." It is easy to follow an example when the example knows the way, goes the way, and shows the way. Example is caught more than it is taught. Parents not only teach by words, but their actions portray much more.

It is imperative that our lives show that Christ is who we say He is. There is no greater injustice than when our actions contradict what we say. A godly example is so important for children to have a stable homelife. Our lives must exemplify that "God is the Head of our home, the unseen Guest at every meal, and the Silent Listener to every conversation." Since God is the Head of the home, parents have a perfect example to follow. God never asks us to do anything he does not help us to carry out. The goal of every parent should be to point the children to God and help them to follow Him gladly.

Faith is the sixth pillar. Hebrews 11:6 teaches us that without faith it is impossible to please [God]. Genuine faith studies and lives the Bible. Faith has a pure heart. "Blessed are the pure in heart: for they shall see God [in everything]" (Matthew 5:8).

Faith can be described as seeing God's hand in everything, and then leaving everything in God's hand. Children are quick to sense whether parents have a heart of faith or whether they have only a head knowledge. The greatest barrier to sharing faith with the children is when we acknowledge Christ with our words, but our minds and hearts are preserved for self and the earthly things. "For where your treasure is, there will your heart be also" (Matthew 6:21). "For with the heart man believeth unto righteousness; and with the mouth confession is made unto salvation" (Romans 10:10).

Parents may say they believe, but the habits of the heart will reveal how sincere and authentic their faith really is. If parents model genuine faith, children are much more apt to grow up to have a reverent and holy fear of God. But the reverse is also true.

The seventh pillar is the *freedom to grow* and become all that God has planned for the child. Even though this is a lifetime process, it begins with the preciousness and innocence of childhood.

There are many things parents learn right along with their children. As the family is established more firmly on the solid foundation of Jesus Christ, they grow together in the likeness of God. Parents will allow, and even encourage, the children to grow from dependence to independence as they become interdependent on God.

It is sad when youth go through school and still cannot read or write properly. It is much sadder when children "graduate" from childhood only to discover they do not know how to live.

The depth of despair or the fullness of joy are two opposites. Which are you parents choosing for your children?

A holy life
is a
whole life.

Blessed are the Parents

Blessed are the parents who make their peace with spilled milk and mud, for of such is the kingdom of childhood.

Blessed are the parents who refuse to compare their children with others, for precious unto each is the rhythm of his own growth.

Blessed are the mothers and fathers, who have learned to laugh, for it is the music of the child's world.

Blessed are those parents who understand the goodness of time, for they make it not a sword that kills growth, but a shield to protect and guide their children.

Blessed are those parents who accept the awkwardness of their growing children, letting each grow at his own speed.

Blessed are the parents who can say "no" without anger, for comforting to the child is the security of a firm decision.

Blessed are the parents who are teachable, for knowledge brings understanding and understanding brings love.

Blessed are the parents who love their children in the midst of a hostile world, for love is the greatest of all gifts.

—Author Unknown
Pulpit Helps
published by AMG Publishers
Chattanooga, TN 37422

22

Communication Bridges the Gap

An interesting conversation was overheard as two first graders were discussing the field trip they were planning to take to a large hospital. One child said, "I don't want to tour the hospital, because I'm scared." To this statement the other one replied, "I'm not scared, that is where nurses take good care of tiny babies, and very sick people can rest and sleep." It was obvious one child knew what a hospital was like, because he had been there with his parents.

Bridging the generation gap is a one-way street. Only as parents teach and familiarize their children with all ages and the realities of life, can children have a proper concept of life.

There is an interesting, yet very sad account of a father-son relationship recorded in II Samuel 13-18. King David encountered many difficult situations, even though he was known as "the man after [God's] own heart" (Acts 13:22b). He had several wives, and of course that meant many children. It was in such a setting that Solomon and Absalom grew up. Each had a different mother, but it is possible they were about the same age. They could have been rivals.

God told King David that Solomon would be his successor, but Absalom gained the attention of the people and falsely informed them he would improve the administration of justice in their best interest. Perhaps Absalom was starving for his father's undivided love and approval. By evil actions he finally got his father's attention. Instead of disciplining Absalom for wrongdoing, King David rejected his son. Absalom did not see the king's face, so he fled and didn't see or talk to his father for two years (II Samuel 14:28). How sad! Instead of communicating and bridging the generation gap, each went his own way and built a wall of indifference that finally led to rebellion. Eventually Absalom proclaimed himself king; then his father fled for his life, because he feared his own son.

In the course of time Absalom was killed (II Samuel 18:15). When David received the report of his death, he mourned uncontrollably. How much better it would have been if the relationship between father and son could have been restored. Finally in desperation, Joab, David's trusted captain, reprimanded him sharply for his unbecoming behavior.

Heartache and fear are the by product of severed relationships. These can be avoided if there is open communication between those who are involved.

We do not need to despair. Rather, we need to learn from stories in the Bible. God has given us ample instruction on how to build good relationships and to communicate with our children so there will be no barriers.

Proverbs 23:17 says, "Be thou in the fear of the LORD all the day long." "The fear of the LORD is the beginning of knowledge" (Proverbs 1:7). "Train up a child in the way he should go: and when he is old, he will not depart from it" (Proverbs 22:6). Bridging the gap begins with a proper concept of God, and regular communication with Him. When parents live in obedience to God, they will be able to instill the fear of God and obedience to Him in their children. "And this is life eternal, that they [our children] might know thee the only true God, and Jesus Christ, whom thou hast sent" (John 17:3).

King Solomon was known as a king with an under-standing heart (I Kings 3:9). We, like Solomon, must ask God often for an understanding heart in order to communi-cate with our children not only by words, but by our lives, attitudes, and actions as well.

From the beginning, God wisely planned for security in the home: one husband, one wife, and children (Genesis 1:27, 28 and Mark 10: 6-9). Parents are commanded by God to teach their children so that they will become godly, responsible, and accountable men and women (Deuteronomy 6:7-9; 11:18-21; Ephesians 6:1-4). During these few years from babyhood to adulthood, much needs to be taught. We need to be sympathetic and considerate. An occasional backward look will help us remember how we felt when we were children. God meets our needs for understanding and compassion (Psalm 103:13) in the way we should meet our children's needs.

When children express hurts and frustrations, we do well to listen and encourage them. We must pray with and for our children, and point them to God's unchanging Word (Matthew 3:6).

Answering children's questions openly and honestly is very important. We may not have all the answers, but we must be humble enough to say, "I don't know, but I'll ask someone who does." This will help avoid that gap that will develop if parents are not honest. Children are quick to detect fraud.

God has promised wisdom if we ask, "If any [parent]

lack wisdom, let [them] ask of God, that giveth . . . liberally" (James 1:5). We must search the Scriptures (John 5:39). The Bible has an answer for our every need.

Bridging the generation gap takes time, lots of time, with our children. Too many parents are too busy making a living or following their own pursuits to communicate properly the true values in life to their children. Their nonverbal communication, actions, and attitudes drive the children to indifference, and finally to rebellion. Years later, when parents are older and children are grown, there is a generation gap that has been widening all along. Many parents mourn because too late they recognize the years were wasted that should have been spent communicating and teaching their children.

Children do not learn to associate with people of all ages without encouragement. The human tendency is to live only for self, but children must be taught to be respectful to the aged, the sick, and special children.

Parents should involve the children when visiting elderly neighbors or church families. Children need to learn to be sensitive to the elderly by doing small jobs, like taking in the mail, or running errands for them without pay. When visiting, encourage the children to take a handful of wild flowers or a picture they drew or colored. Help them by suggesting they take a piece of cake or pie. At times small children may be frightened by the elderly, but with open communication their fears will vanish. Bringing cheer to the shut-in can give children a sense of worth. Encourage them by singing a song and offering a prayer for their protection. Visiting others together is a sure way of bridging the generation gap.

The importance of families visiting the elderly and sick was impressed upon us several years ago. My stepfather was sick and needed to be hospitalized for ten days. He then died soon afterwards. A young family with several children visited him in the hospital on two occasions. The family brought cheer and comfort to the dying man. The children had numerous questions, and the parents patiently answered all of them. The children were not afraid because their parents instilled a love for people, no matter their age. These parents also helped their children grasp the reality of aging and finally death. When the family came to the viewing and visitation before the funeral, the children knew who had died, and this helped them be confident and calm.

Another couple with several children was also at the same viewing and visitation. When they met the family of the deceased, their six-year-old was wide-eyed and looked shocked. Seemingly, questions were written all over his face as he looked from the deceased to the family. He had no idea there was any connection.

When there is a sick friend or if one dies, include your children. Talk to them about death. Help them to realize it is a gateway to glory, if one is ready to meet God. Help them also to realize that unless Jesus comes soon, we will all face death.

By carefully teaching and communicating with our families, we are building bridges that will close any gaps between generations that may appear.

A Recipe for Happiness

Happiness is something we create in our minds.
It's not something you search for and seldom find . . .
By counting our blessings, and kneeling to pray . . .
It's giving up thoughts that breed discontent
And accepting what comes as a "gift heaven-sent."
It's giving up wishing for things we have not
And making the best of whatever we've got . . .
It's knowing that life is determined for us,
And pursuing our tasks without fret or fuss . . .
For it's by completing what God gives us to do
That we find real contentment and happiness too.

—Author Unknown

23
Tell the Children

Imagine, with me, what an evening in ancient Israel consisted of. The day's work is done, the evening meal cleared away, and the family is sitting around a crude table in a tent made of animal skins. There is no electricity, only an unpolished rough candle or perhaps a small lamp. There are no evening meetings to attend, no books to read, no newspaper or amusements. An evening in ancient Israel consisted of talking together as a family. There was no Bible to turn to for bedtime stories. Telling the children was the only way to convey important events. It was the only way to transmit God's wonderful works to the next generation. "One generation shall praise thy works to another, and shall declare thy mighty acts" (Psalm 145:4).

Storytelling was very important, and it was the father's responsibility to share with the children (Deuteronomy 6:1-13).

Imagine how it would be to listen to a father as he relates the story of the Creation and the account of Adam and Eve in the beautiful garden. Then he tells of the sad happening when Cain killed his brother Abel, all because of envy and jealousy.

The grandparents may have lived in the same tent with the family. At times Grandpa may relate stories. He may tell of Noah and his three sons who built a big boat on dry ground; then later it rained and the land creatures outside the ark drowned.

One story that must have fascinated the children was the story of Joseph. He was sincere and obedient to his father, and yet his brothers despised him. Later, the brothers sold him to strangers that were passing from Canaan to Egypt. As Grandfather relates the story, the children straighten their tired shoulders in order to get all the details. God had a wonderful plan, even though Joseph went through many sad times.

When Father told the story of the exodus from Egypt, they were eager to hear all the details, because many of them were born during the forty years of wandering in the wilderness.

Countless stories were related and many were favorites of the children. Perhaps they asked for the same ones over and over again. Since this was the only way of communicating, it was imperative that every point be accurate.

Very solemnly Grandfather and Father instructed the children of the importance of obedience as they recalled the account of Moses striking the rock rather than speaking to it as God commanded. They also explained the numerous times God punished the Israelites because of disobedience.

One time especially stood out to Father. It was when Aaron made a golden calf and all the people were feasting and dancing while Moses was on the mountain where God gave him the Ten Commandments. He recalls how bitter the water was that they needed to drink because they disobeyed and disappointed God.

Now centuries later, it is just as pertinent to tell the children. How will the children know the truth unless parents tell them?

Psalm 77:14:   "Thou art the God that doest wonders." This statement is just as true today as it was when Asaph penned these words; but unless we tell the children, they will not know.

Too many people depend on others—the news media, the church, or school—to tell the children. But God has placed this responsibility squarely on the shoulders of parents. "And, ye fathers, provoke not your children to wrath: but bring them up in the nurture and admonition of the Lord" (Ephesians 6:4). In other words, God is commanding parents to educate their children in God's ways.

It takes wisdom from God to know how and when to teach the children, and there are always requirements that must be met. The first mandate is to love the Lord and know Him personally. He must be Lord and Master of the parents' life before they can instill proper respect and love for God in the children's hearts. God's blessings and His will must be real in the lives of parents in order to tell their children, the wonderful works of God. "We will not hide them from their children, shewing to the generation to come the praises of the LORD and his strength, and his wonderful works that he hath done" (Psalm 78:4).

In the Old Testament, Aaron and his sons were priests (I Chronicles 23:13). Priests were those who stood between God and man and offered sacrifices to God daily. I Chronicles 23:30-31b says they stood "every morning to thank and praise the Lord, and likewise at even . . . according to the order commanded unto them, continually before the LORD." What a priest was in the tabernacle is what godly parents are to God for their families "to present every [family member] perfect" before God (Colossians 1:28).

Job was another example of a priest to his family. "Job sent and sanctified [his children], and rose up early in the morning, and offered [prayers] according to the number of them all: for Job said, It may be that my [children] have sinned, and cursed God in their hearts. Thus did Job continually" (Job 1:5). In ancient days it was only a sanctified heart that could present a burnt offering and prayers to a holy God.

Parents in our present day must also have holy and pure hearts in order to relate God's wonderful Truth to the children.

Since parents stand between God and their children much as the priest did in the tabernacle, it is imperative that they convey a holy concept of God. Priests were sometimes called servants, because of their work. Isaiah 61:6: "But ye shall be named the Priests of the LORD: men shall call you the [servants] of our God." Parents with servant hearts will be able to portray God's love to the children.

When parents fail to tell the children, it is because they do not have a proper concept of God themselves; therefore they cannot share the Truth about God and life in its sacredness.

After Gypsy Smith had been preaching for over fifty years, someone asked him how he can still have the same fervor for God. His answer was, "I have never lost the wonder of it all."

In parents' zeal to tell their children, no one dare lose the amazement, wonder, and admiration for God.

Grandparents, too, have many opportunities to convey the wonders of God. There is beauty all around, if only eyes are open to see. Show the children the perfectly built robin nest and point out the tiny blue eggs. Help the children respect the baby birds as they hatch, grow, and finally leave the nest.

Bring their attention to a beautiful flower bud, or help

them pick some wild flowers (even if they are weeds) and enjoy the small arrangement for a day or two.

Tell the children about the diligence of an ant, and show them the double or triple weight an ant is able to carry. Remind them what the Bible says about the ant. Proverbs 6:6: "Go to the ant, thou sluggard; consider her ways, and be wise." Proverbs 30:25: "The ants are a people not strong, yet they prepare their meat in the summer."

Children are eager to learn, and they must be taught to be alert and observant. Pointing out little insignificant details of life will open communication. If parents and grandparents take time to answer the questions honestly, often these questions lead to questions concerning the sanctity and purity of life.

Read Bible stories and character-building stories to the children and grandchildren. It certainly opens doors of communication. They will feel more at ease to ask questions when they are aware that the stories we tell them are the same as are found in God's Word.

There may be times at an early age that children will not always tell the truth, but be honest and teach the importance of telling the truth and being totally honest. Bring God into focus as much as possible, reminding them God sees and hears. This is the beginning of instilling the fear of God in their lives as they grow older.

Children love stories of their parents' experiences as youth. Sad stories need to be shared perhaps with regret as well as how victory is gained.

While we are telling our children, there may be times our actions speak louder than our words.

In I Corinthians 11:1, Paul could rightfully encourage his followers to follow him as he followed Christ because he knew the value of consistent living.

It has been said that children can stand a vast amount of sternness, but it is injustice, inequity, and inconsistency that kills them.

From the children's earliest infancy, instill the necessity of prompt obedience. Unite firmness with gentleness. Let the children know you mean what you say and that you say what you mean.

At times it is very helpful to have the child's full attention. Use eye contact when you give instructions. If it is needful, show the children how you want a certain thing done, then see to it that it is accomplished.

Obedience and communications were imperative in ancient Israel. And it is sad, but it is very lacking in the twentieth century.

Ephesians 6:1 instructs us, "Children, obey your parents in the Lord: for it is right."

It is of utmost importance that parents love and obey God, and that reverence permeates the lives of parents in order to pass on this much-needed principle to the generations to come.

Tell the children. Communicate with them. Teach them obedience, for "a child left to himself bringeth his mother to shame" (Proverbs 29:15).

A home that is blessed
with trust and true love,
is fashioned with care
by the Lord up above.

Commitment involves

- *wholehearted allegiance to God with no rights to myself, (Matthew 22:37-39),*
- *saying God's will be done, (Matthew 26:39),*
- *seeing God's hand in every circumstance, (Matthew 5:8),*
- *seeing obstacles through to completion, (II Timothy 4:7),*
- *loving rather than being partial, (James 2:2, 3),*
- *viewing life from God's perspective, (Psalm 39:4),*
- *not allowing the urgent to exceed the important (Matthew 6:33),*
- *total devotion to Jesus as Lord, not devoted to service (Matthew 6:33),*
- *guarding my heart with great diligence because it is the reservoir of the mind (Proverbs 4:23),*
- *keeping strict guard of my lips, (Psalm 141:3).*

Rewards of Commitment are

- *an inner joy and peace that my life pleases God (Isaiah 26:3),*
- *knowing my name is written in heaven (Luke 10:20),*
- *recognizing God rewards faithfulness (II Chronicles 15:7),*
- *an eternal home in heaven (Romans 6:23).*

24
Carefully Pass the Baton

God calls on His people to pass the faith on from one generation to the next. This can be likened to running in a relay where one runner passes the baton to the next one. God has had, and still has, faithful athletes in the race.

Amram and Jochebed lived under the harsh reign of King Amasa, the founder of the eighteenth dynasty in Egypt. There was something special about this couple. They were dedicated to God and had a deep concern for their children. They were concerned that they pass the baton on to the next generation. They also noticed when their third child was born that he was a goodly child (Exodus 2:2).

The king had sent a decree to the Israelites that every baby boy who was born should be thrown into the Nile River, but the girls were permitted to live (Exodus 1:22).

Imagine the apprehension when the midwife announced that God had blessed them with a healthy baby boy. The Bible tells us the family hid their baby three months. All the while it was a prayerful and careful family that kept pleading with God to keep their baby safe.

One day God gave Jochebed an idea that would work. She sent Aaron and Miriam to gather bulrushes from the riverside. She made a small waterproof basket, carefully placed her precious baby boy into the soft bed, and carried him to the river. Big sister Miriam was stationed close by to see what would become of her little brother.

Sometime later, the king's daughter and her maids came to the river to refresh themselves. The princess noticed the strange-looking basket floating among the reeds.

When one of her maids brought the basket to the princess, the baby cried. This touched the king's daughter's heart. She knew it was one of the Israelite babies whom her father had ordered to be killed.

God had it all planned, and the princess made plans to adopt this baby. Sister Miriam was available to find a nurse for the princess. She ran home quickly to bring the good news to the family. Pharaoh's daughter named him Moses because she drew him out of the water (Exodus 2:10b).

Now baby Moses didn't need to stay hidden any longer. No doubt, his parents were quick to inform others they were caring for the baby until he was old enough to leave his mother (Exodus 2:9, 10).

Just as Moses' parents took seriously the responsibility of another baby, so must every couple take very seriously the responsibility of parenthood. All children are precious. Children are gifts from God to be taught and trained for God's glory and for His service.

Children are merely lent to parents for a short time. Parents need to be just as diligent as Moses' parents were in teaching them about God and His purposes for their lives, because every child is "goodly." This Hebrew adjective means "good, beneficial, well-favored, and right." Moses' parents influenced him so deeply that years later he "chose rather to suffer affliction with the people of God then to enjoy the pleasures of sin for a season" (Hebrews 11:24-26). Moses' early childhood training, perhaps only his first five or seven years, made such an indelible impression on him that he was more concerned about God's will than his own selfish ambitions.

Amram and Jochebed were successful in cautiously handing the baton to their children. God is still requiring parents to teach and instill His Word into the hearts of their children so well that the baton can safely be handed to them.

Either people live by God's principles or they ignore His principles. In Paul's writings, he refers to the Christian marathon, a race of great length and one of endurance. He mentions "running the race with patience" (Hebrews 12:1, 2); and "pressing toward the mark for the prize" (Philippians 3:14).

Ecclesiastes 9:11 reminds us "the race is not to the swift." If the race were lost, it was not for lack of speed, but rather because of failure to smoothly pass on the baton. A baton is "a hollow cylinder carried by each member of the team and passed on successfully to the succeeding runner" (Webster). Moses' parents were a good example of successfully passing the baton to their children.

Noah is another example. He and his whole family were saved during the Flood, by his obedience and faithfulness. God said, "Come thou and all thy house into the ark; for thee have I seen righteous before me in this generation" (Genesis 7:1). Verse 5 gives us the secret of Noah's success in carefully passing the baton: "And Noah did according unto all that the Lord commanded."

By way of contrast, Lot was a failure. He lost his whole family except his two daughters. Even his wife looked back and became a pillar of salt (Genesis 19:16, 26). He lacked the qualities necessary for passing the baton.

Eli was a priest of God, and yet he failed as a parent (I Samuel 2:22-26). Verse 24 tells us he chided his sons but did not command obedience. He did not restrain them; therefore God withheld his blessings from Eli's house forever (I Samuel 3:13, 14).

God has given us instructions for carefully passing the baton. In Deuteronomy 6:5-9, we are commanded to love the LORD our God with all our heart and soul and might. God expects us to hide His Word in our hearts. Then we are able to teach His principles and commandments diligently to our children.

Diligence is imperative! Teaching children cannot be done half-heartedly or while we are half asleep or engrossed in our material pursuits.

God tells us to teach constantly—while we are working, sitting in our home, while we walk or travel, before we go to bed, and as soon as we get up in the morning. We are always teaching whether we are aware of it or not.

Our lives need to be so full of God that we see Him working in circumstances and in every-day situations. Only then is it possible really to relate to our children the wonderful works of God. Even when our schedules are changed, if we see God as the One who plans and directs our lives, it will be easy to convey this to our children. Matthew 5:8, "Blessed are the pure in heart: for they shall see God [in everything]." When prayer is a vital ingredient in the home and the family prays together for a certain need, and God answers that need, God's answer becomes a memorial of God's goodness to us.

Posting Bible verses to memorize serves as "frontlets" to our eyes. One young mother of preschool children has helped the children to memorize whole psalms by pictures. Little children can read by pictures before they are able to read words. Adults as well as children need continual reminders because we may forget the Lord (verse 12).

"Except the LORD build the house, they labour in vain that build it; except the LORD keep the city, the watchman waketh but in vain" (Psalm 127:1).

Parents dare not wait to build a good relationship until the teen years. It must be established at a very young age. Susannah Wesley once said, "I get hold of my child's heart and never lose its grip."

God's promises are for all ages, for all people. "I am with thee and will keep thee in all places whither thou goest . . . I will not leave thee."

Paul in Ephesians 6:10-18, gives the description of one who is able to pass the baton successfully to the ongoing generations. "Finally, my brethren, be strong in the Lord and in the the power of His might. Put on the whole armour of God, that ye may be able to stand against the wiles of the devil."

- We must be covered by God's truth.
- We must have a breastplate of righteousness, which is found only as Jesus makes us righteous.
- God commands us to share the saving message of Jesus; therefore we must be shod with the Gospel of peace.
- Believing in Jesus is the shield of faith. It is being aware that God is and knowing He is in complete control of life.
- Salvation is the helmet. It is knowing our sins are forgiven, and we live with eternity in view.
- We must hide God's Word in our hearts by meditation and memorization. "His delight is in the law of the LORD; and in his law doth he meditate day and night" (Psalm 1:2). God's Word is the sword of the Spirit. Satan is defeated when we use it effectively.
- Finally, we must be "praying always with prayer and

supplication in the spirit."

We are running in a race, a relay in which one must pass the baton to the next runner. As we are faithful and endure, we can be found worthy to pass on the baton of faith to the coming generations.

"I press toward the mark for the prize of the high calling of God in Christ Jesus" (Philippians 3:14).

The highest quality
of service comes
from the deepest
devotion to God.

As an eagle stirreth up her nest, fluttereth over her young, spreadeth abroad her wings, taketh them, beareth them on her wings: so the Lord alone [leads us] (Deuteronomy 32:11, 12).

CHANGE, THANKS, GOD

*I don't want
to face
it.
I'm comfortable
just the way
I am.
But
God
shakes my world
and I'm forced
to hold on
to Him.
I cry out
in pain, but
as I struggle
I find
wings.*

*On reaching new heights
I look back
and say,
"Thanks, God."
You shook my nest
with love,
because you
care.*

*Mary Anna Swarey
used by permission 1998*

25

Children Need
Roots and Wings

Hotting Carter once said, "There are two lasting virtues we can give to our children. One of these is roots and the other wings."

God is expecting parents, especially mothers, to be the stabilizing factor in equipping the children with both of these. She is to be supportive without being pushy. She needs to stay within reach, yet she dare not be demanding or insistent. She can be an inspiration, as children learn from her strong and realistic performance in everyday life. She gives both stability and courage. She provides healthy roots by teaching the children how to build their lives upon the firm foundation of God's Word, His values, and His promises. Psalm 11:3 says, "If the foundations be destroyed, what can the righteous do?"

She plants the children firmly among God's people. Her prayers and unconditional love guide them in the way they should go, and when they are old, they will not depart from it (Proverbs 22:6).

Webster's dictionary defines roots as: "a means of anchorage, an underlying support; an ultimate or fundamental source not easily discerned."

The Joshua tree, according to the *World Book* is one of the few trees that can tolerate the desert climate because their roots go deep into the earth, as far as 150 feet in search of food and moisture. This is the kind of roots we must provide for our children. The world is sometimes referred to as a desert. Our children's roots must reach deep into God's truth.

There are two kinds of roots described in the Bible. One kind is the root of bitterness "lest there should be among you a root that beareth gall and wormwood [or poisonous herbs]" (Deuteronomy 29:18).

We must "[look] diligently lest [we] fail of the grace of God; lest any root of bitterness springing up trouble [us], and thereby many be defiled" (Hebrews 12:15).

The other kind of root is the Root of Jesse, referring to Jesus. "And in that day there shall be a root of Jesse, which shall stand as an ensign [emblem or sign] for the people; to it shall the Gentiles seek: and his rest shall be glorious" (Isaiah 11:10).

Jesus is the Root, that true foundation on which we must build, in order for our children's roots to be well grounded.

And as for wings, the mother can instill a deep faith in God—the One who created each child for His eternal purpose and for His glory. Mother can also instill the courage children need in order to try, and try again. Children need to hear, "I know you can." When they make mistakes, the mother needs to reassure them, "Don't be afraid. Try again. I also make mistakes." This stills the fear that is threatening to overpower them.

Each child needs to know his parents accept him as a unique person, an individual, not a carbon copy. Children need to be told there is no one in all the world exactly like them, and God has also assigned a unique work for them that no one else can fill as God would desire them to. This frees the child to take a deep breath, spread his wings, and soar.

God cared for the children of Israel as the eagle cares for its young. "As an eagle stirreth up her nest, fluttereth over her young, spreadeth abroad her wings, taketh them, beareth them on her wings" (Deuteronomy 32:11). The eagle is observed to have a strong affection for her young, protecting them and making provision for them, educating them and teaching them to fly. This provides an example for parents in the training of their children as they lead them into godly living.

Perhaps mothers also need to do like the eagle—make the nest a bit uncomfortable and push their young out of the nest. Like the eagle, a mother won't let them fall to their death; she, too, spreads her wings and bears them up to try again. She carries them and encourages them until they have learned the art of flying, and finally, soaring.

As a mother exercises godly wisdom and understanding, she can encourage her children to spread their wings. "Get wisdom, get understanding" (Proverbs 4:5). "Wisdom is the principal thing; therefore get wisdom: and with all thy getting get understanding" (Proverbs 4:7). "The fear of the Lord is the beginning of knowledge" (Proverbs 1:7).

Mothers must be optimistic as well as realistic. They can challenge children to greater heights, but should not expect more than they can perform. If goals are not achieved, they should not be overly critical. Many a child's vision has been dampened by a negative comment or discouraging word.

In preparing our children "to endure hardness as a good soldier of Jesus Christ" (II Timothy 2:3), we need to nurture in them deep roots like those of the Joshua tree, so they can endure the desert storms in which they are called to live. They also need wings like an eagle in order to soar to the heights of God's potential.

As we free them, we need to bow our heads humbly and ask God to make our children all He desires for them to become.

Both roots and wings are essential!

We never
lose what we
offer to Christ.

A Woman from God's Perspective

A godly woman has a meek and quiet spirit. She has learned to accept the circumstances in which God has placed her. She has a contented spirit. Life does not have to be perfect for her to be happy. A woman with this spirit radiates an inner beauty that is truly attractive.

26
Aging, Yet Ageless

Aging yet ageless, what a paradox! We know that age is different stages of life. Webster defines age as becoming mellow or mature, to bring to a state fit for use.

Ageless means timeless and eternal. We are aging, yet we will live on forever.

There are jokes made about aging such as "out of the way" or "over the hill." But from God's perspective, life should be getting more serious, more earnest, more pious and devoted. Generally this is what takes place. Either we become more Christ-like and more fulfilled, or we become somber and gloomy. Either we become more competent and confident in God's grace, or we become more fearful and irritable. It all depends on our attitudes early in life.

Charles Swindoll made this statement, "I am convinced that life is 10% what happens to me and 90% how I react to it. We are in charge of our attitudes."

"Lord, make me to know my end, [and to appreciate the days you allow me to live] . . . let me know how [very weak] I am" (Psalm 39:4, 5 paraphrased). Recognizing the Lord as the sustainer of the universe and realizing the very breath of life is a gift from God bring proper perspective to aging. Life and aging is a gift from God. We need to show by discretion that we believe we are responsible for how we live.

"Making the most of time—buying up each opportunity" (Ephesians 5:16 Amplified). God expects us to invest our life in the pursuit of eternity. Our lifestyle is an unconscious reflection of our conviction. The quality of life declares true identity.

Wherever you are, "Be all there," was Jim Elliot's goal. His life was a reflection of this, as he so diligently followed God. He well knew that no matter how long he could serve God, he would live eternally; therefore, he lived with purpose.

A number of ageless wonders include those who enjoyed life in their fifties and sixties, or even later in life.

Helen Steiner Rice compiled many of her poems in her older years.

Catherine Marshall wrote a number of books.

Fannie Crosby composed many hymns even in her older age.

Look forward to the fifties and aging as a challenge. But we must remember the pattern of our thinking is fashioned during youth and mid-life.

Be enthusiastic! The Greek word means inspired or possessed by God. David, the writer of many of the psalms, was enthusiastic. An enthusiastic spirit will spare us from discouragement in circumstances in which the nominal Christian would despair. Being controlled by God's Spirit is another definition for enthusiasm.

Jesus, our perfect example, was possessed by the Holy Spirit, and no one on earth was more enthusiastic. He was never self-motivated. His passions were always under the control of His Father in Heaven.

Those who center their lives on God will be enthusiastic for the things of God. "But seek ye first the Kingdom of God...and all these things shall be added unto you"

(Matthew 6:33). "For where your treasure is, there will your heart be also" (Matthew 6:21).

Enthusiasm rejoices in the God of our salvation. Being enthusiastic is a service to others. "Whatsoever ye do, do it heartily as to the Lord" (Colossians 3:23). We are to be "always abounding in the work of the Lord" (I Corinthians 15:58).

Enthusiasm turns self-pity and complaining to praise, and grumbling to gratitude. Enthusiasm is the key to releasing all the energies of God, but this virtue is not always easy to attain. It takes perseverance! It also takes a proper attitude—an attitude of gratitude that has been developed during the formative years.

Be an encourager! "[Encourage] one another daily" (Hebrews 3:13). In order to encourage, we must be committed to reading and studying God's Word. Strive to become all God would have you to become. Commit your daily life to be one of victory, because Jesus is the Victor!

There are many opportunities available to one who is willing to be an encourager. All ages are blessed by an occasional word of commendation.

Teenagers need someone who has been a teenager and who remembers with compassion the trials and pressures teens face. They need to know older ones not only survived the teen years, but are thriving in the later, but more rewarding phase of life.

Young mothers with preschool children need assistance. Give them an encouraging word. More than that, give them several hours of quiet time by entertaining the children, so they can rekindle their commitment to God and to the ever-demanding needs of babies and toddlers. Whatever you do, be all there!

The elderly need a listening ear. Perhaps they need

someone to wash their windows or take them shopping. Often their only way of communication is by telephone. Be sensitive. Be an encourager!

Submission is also an important area in growing older. James 4:6 reminds us to submit to God." Accepting our age and recognizing we do have limitations will contribute to a fulfilled life. Sometime ago I was talking to one whose youngest child reached school age. When I asked her what she does now that the baby is in school, she replied, "Oh, it takes so much longer to do things than when I was younger." That is true, but don't waste time. Be enthusiastic!

James 4:8 reminds us to "draw nigh to God, and he will draw nigh to [us]." As we gratefully accept our limitations, we become more aware that God's grace is sufficient (II Corinthians 12:9). In our weakness and limitations, God desires to become our strength.

We must be careful that we do not allow past blessings and youthful energies to keep us from being useful in later years. I praise God, He has been with me through every phase of life. I would never have made it without His all-sufficient help.

As we enter the glorious age, aging, yet ageless, we certainly owe our whole life to our Creator, whether the years be few or many. God deserves all our praise and glory.

Faith is another characteristic of one who is aging, yet recognizes that he is ageless. Faith does not deny reality. It does not immune us to pain. Neither does faith remove trials and difficulties. Rather, faith in God brings God into each situation. Only God can give us a proper perspective. He always works for our eternal good (Romans 8:28). When our focus is on God, it does not so much change the situation as it changes our perspective.

Exodus 23:20, has a promise for the aging, yet ageless. "Behold, I send an Angel before thee, to keep thee in the way [of aging], and to bring thee into the place which I have prepared [eternity]."

A woman with an empty nest will have more hours to fill. I write this with due respect. With age comes slower thinking, tottering steps and less than supple hands. The whole body is not as keen and alert as earlier in life. But there will be hours that need to be filled with something edifying and worthwhile. We do well to prepare for this as we go through the thirties and forties.

Sometimes in order to see life more clearly, we need to do some comparing. Here is where a backward look is in order.

A mother with four children, has her alarm set for 6:00 a.m. Thirty-five years later the alarm still sounds at 6:00 a.m. For a family of six to have a solid breakfast and family devotions together in a relaxed way, will mean at least two or more hours. There are lunches to pack and the husband needs to prepare for his work.

Since it's just Bennie and I, within two hours we've enjoyed a solid breakfast, family devotions, the dishes done, lunch prepared, laundry done, and I am ready for my private devotions and to begin the day's activities.

Instead of two or three large loads of daily laundry, I now have two small loads. Instead of washing dishes for a family of six, I only have several utensils and dishes.

I have been blessed as I plan ahead. I still fix several pounds of hamburger, pork, and chicken. I either freeze individual servings, or fix several plates. I also bake bars or a cake, and cut and wrap pieces individually and freeze for later.

Again in the evening, let us compare time as a couple or

a family of six. Everyone is gone all day. At 4:00 p.m., the school children arrive. Perhaps the husband is home by 4:00 p.m. It will again take several hours to prepare a balanced meal and clean up the kitchen properly afterward.

With just the two of us, since our main meal is at noon, we enjoy soup or sandwiches for supper. Imagine looking at the clock at 5:45 p.m., supper over, dishes washed, and the kitchen tidy. What now?

For me there is more time. I am reminded of Jesus' words in Luke 12:48 "For unto whomsoever much is given, of him shall be much required: and to whom men have committed much, of him ask they more." God holds us responsible for the time He has so graciously given us.

In one of our church papers, I found an interesting interview concerning aging, yet ageless. This pastor of forty-five years had a proper perspective. When asked why he didn't sit back and take it easy he replied, "Where I live we have two distinct types of seniors. The one group serves in various volunteer programs. The other group is here to golf, gobble, and gab. Guess who is more depressed! I prefer to think of aging as a period of transition. I am now able to do things I did not have time to do before."

Brother Wiebe made aging sound almost desirable. Aging is inevitable, but it can be a life of opportunities, when you consider the alternative. He further states that aging clarifies values. We are able to see more clearly what is really important, endless, and eternal.

When asked how he maintains his upbeat attitude, he replied, "I am fortunate to have optimism in the genes. I have also been inspired by other saints who have a proper attitude." Optimism can be developed by seeing from God's perspective.

The aging Christian can honestly say, "I enjoyed my

younger days, but I have no desire to stay young. Each step is one step closer HOME!"

Consider our lives consumable for Christ, our reasonable service, a living sacrifice (Romans 12:1, 2). By example we must teach the joy of putting Jesus first and others before ourselves. We give our lives in service for others rather than seeing others as opportunities to aid our own advancement.

By example, we set our goal, not necessarily to get ahead, but rather, to enlarge God's kingdom.

We may feel like the woman in Mark 12:41-44. She placed two mites into the offering and Jesus took notice. He observed she gave all her living. One mite, plus one mite, plus true devotion, equals everything in Christ.

The Christian Family

The Christian family is a blessing—
When each member does his part;
And our care for each other,
Comes from God's love in our heart!

The Christian family is a blessing—
When the father sees the need;
To instruct and teach his children,
From God's Word—and thus takes heed!

The Christian family is a blessing—
When the mother fills her role;
And her words are kind and loving,
When Christ Jesus has control!

The Christian family is a blessing—
When each child obeys the Lord;
To respect, obey thy parents,
Is commanded in God's Word!

The Christian family is a blessing—
When we all God's will fulfill;
Then our love will blossom daily,
In the center of God's will!

Mrs. Martha King
used by permission 1999

You Can Find Our Books at These Stores:

GEORGIA
Montezuma
  The Family Book Shop
  912/472-5166

INDIANA
Lagrange
  Pathway Bookstore
Wakarusa
  Maranatha Christian
    Bookstore
  219/862-4332

IOWA
Kalona
  Friendship Bookstore

KENTUCKY
Harrodsburg
  Kountry Kupboard
  814/629-1588
Stephensport
  Martin's Bookstore
  270/547-4206

LOUISIANA
Belle Chasse
  Good News Bookstore
  540/394-3087

MARYLAND
Union Bridge
  Home Ties
  410/775-2511

MICHIGAN
Eveart
  Hillview Books and Fabric
  231/734-3394
Fremont
  Helping Hand Home
  231/924-0041
Snover
  Country View Store
  517/635-3764

MISSOURI
Rutledge
  Zimmerman's Store
  660/883-5766
St. Louis
  The Homeschool Sampler
  314/835-0863
Seymour
  Byler Supply & Country
    Store
  417/935-4522
Versailles
  Excelsior Bookstore
  573/378-1925

OHIO
Berlin
  Gospel Book Store
Hopewell
  Four Winds Bookstore
  740/454-7990
Mesopotamia
  Eli Miller's Leather Shop
  440/693-4448

**Our books may also be found on many
Choice Books Bookracks**

Middlefield
Wayside Merchandise
Books and Gifts

Millersburg
Country Furniture &
Bookstore
330/893-4455

Plain City
Deeper Life Bookstore
614/873-1199

PENNSYLVANIA
Belleville
Yoder's Gospel Book Store
717/483-6697

Ephrata
Clay Book Store
717/733-7253

Conestoga Bookstore
717/354-0475

Guys Mills
Christian Learning
Resource
814/789-4769

Leola
Conestoga Valley Books
Bindery
717/656-8824

McVeytown
Penn Valley Christian
Retreat
717/899-5000

Narvon
Springville Woodworks
856/875-6916

Springboro
Chupp's Country Cupboard
814/587-3678

Stoystown
Kountry Pantry
814/629-1588

TENNESSEE
Crossville
Troyer's Country Cupboard
931/277-5886

TEXAS
Kemp
Heritage Market and
Bakery
903/498-3366

VIRGINIA
Dayton Farmer's Market
Books of Merit
540/879-5013

Harrisonburg
Christian Light
Publications
540/434-0768

Stuarts Draft
The Cheese Shop
540/337-4224

CANADA
British Columbia
 Burns Lake
Wildwood Bibles and
Books
250/698-7451

Ontario
 Brunner
Country Cousins
519/595-4277

**Our books may also be found on many
Choice Books Bookracks**

Order Form

To order, send this completed order form to:

Vision Publishers, Inc.
P.O. Box 190
Harrisonburg, VA 22803
or fax
540-432-6530

_____   _____
Name   Date

_____   _____
Mailing Address   Phone

_____
City   State   Zip

A Woman by God's Grace   Quantity ____ x $8.99 each = _____

A Woman for God's Glory   Quantity ____ x $9.99 each = _____

A Woman from God's Perspective Quantity ____ x $8.99 each = _____

Price _____

Virginia residents add 4.5% sales tax _____

Grand Total _____

All Prices Include Shipping and Handling
❑ Visa   **All Payments in US Dollars**
❑ MasterCard
Card # ❑ ❑ ❑ ❑   ❑ ❑ ❑ ❑   ❑ ❑ ❑ ❑   ❑ ❑ ❑ ❑
Exp. Date ❑ ❑ ❑ ❑

Thank you for your order!

For a complete listing of our books,
write for our catalog.

Bookstore inquiries welcome